A PLACE TO MAKE
MEMORIES

STORIES AND RECIPES FROM
THE LAZY M LODGE

RANDY R MCGHEE

 FriesenPress

Suite 300 - 990 Fort St
Victoria, BC, V8V 3K2
Canada

www.friesenpress.com

Front cover painting by Kate More

ISBN
978-1-5255-4342-5 (Hardcover)
978-1-5255-4343-2 (Paperback)
978-1-5255-4344-9 (eBook)

1. Travel, Canada, Western Provinces (Ab, Bc)

Distributed to the trade by The Ingram Book Company

This book is dedicated to: My partner and best friend Marcel, family, friends and the many guests. You all have inspired and supported me through this writing journey. Without you, I would be still on page one. Thank you for all your contributions.

May this book encourage you to follow your own soul-filling adventure.

July 16 2019

Sandi -

Randy R. mcshea

TABLE OF CONTENTS

THIS IS WHERE WE START. . .

PUTTING PEN TO PAPER IS MORE OF A CHALLENGE THAN ONE CAN IMAGINE.. With support from Marcel, my family, as well as hundreds of guests and friends, I can tell this story. I hope you will enjoy reading our stories and recipes, and how far we have come in five years.

My name is Randy Robert McGhee, the middle son born to Merton and Jean McGhee in March of 1963. With my older brother Stacy, and younger brother, Todd, our home was the Turtle Back Farm just north of the Orkney Community Hall in the small community of Orkney, located west of Drumheller, Alberta,

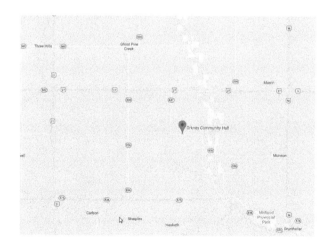

The Turtle Back Farm is just north of the Orkney Community Hall

The farm was homesteaded by my great grandfather, Wyatt W. McGhee in 1907. He brought his wife and seven children to make this part of the world their home. Living in a sod shack until a home could be built, life on the prairie was anything but easy. During the summer, the family worked hard breaking the prairie sod, planting crops, and raising animals.

The women and young children spent winters with relatives in Acme. The winter of 1908-1909, was one of the coldest, and several horses, cattle and small animals froze to death. They overcame this hardship the following year, after spending the winter transporting logs from west of Didsbury to the family farm in order to build two homes, a barn and several out buildings.

This was the beginning of the community that came to be known as Orkney, in honour of the four families who arrived from Orkney Island in Scotland, whom Wyatt McGhee had encouraged that this would be a great place to homestead on the farm..

This group of settlers formed a school district and built a church. This tight-knit community worked together for generations. Several of those original homesteaders still have family still working the land today. Todd McGhee has taken over the Turtle Back Farm, which will always be home to our family.

Turtle Back Farm, aerial view 2004

Turtle Back is a mixed farm with grain, cattle, horses, sheep, and chickens. There were always large gardens and fruit trees. There were endless hours of work, some would say, but life on the farm is what you make it. Our family always found a balance of work and play.

I was very fortunate to be able to attend a one-room schoolhouse for grades one to six, and I have so many memories of this experience. This was the same school my grandfather went to, and I was the last student through the door when it closed in 1975. Mrs. Borwick taught all six grades and she had her hands full with eighteen students. Under the guidance of Mrs. Borwick, I was able to gain credits in school for writing the stories of our pioneers.

The love of my community and its history was the incentive for me to organize all the neighbours and put together a history book. *Orkney History* was published in 1982. The following is an excerpt:

38

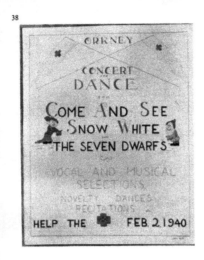

Drawn by Jean (Taylor) Robbie

Orkney Christmas Concert, 1967

THE LAST YEARS AT ORKNEY

by Randy McGhee

The memories of Orkney aren't complete without the memories of our years at school. Everyone has their own special times and experiences which they remember most. But for all of us there is a common set of images, experiences which they remember. I hope to bring some of these to mind by telling of my years at Orkney. Some details will be different for sure, if you attended, say in 1920, but I'm sure you will get the same pictures in your mind as I do.

My first grade at Orkney began in September of 1969, Grant Bergos and I became pupils of Mrs. Norma Borwick. Like all Grade ones before us we had to learn to read, write, add and subtract. It was so exciting to get those big red pencils, new scribblers and books. The first book we had to read was "Tip". Then "Janet and Tip", and then on to harder reading.

Grade One was so exciting and before we knew it we were in Grade two. The first day of school was always scary and exciting. When we arrived we would talk about the summer which was gone forever and the new long, long year ahead of us. Mrs. Borwick would ring the bell, unless someone asked to ring it first - you felt so important if you got to ring the bell! On that first day Mrs. Borwick would get the yard stick out and measure the height of each person's waist to determine the most suitable desk size. Our desks were always neatly arranged in rows, with the teacher's desk in the center, grade ones near the side door, up to grade six who had the prestigious window view.

For the six years I went to Orkney, each day of the week had a set routine that never changed. Frank Trentham, our faithful, fearless bus driver always had us to school at 8:45. As we filed into the school, we set our lunch buckets above the book rack, hung our coats and then into our desks. At nine o'clock Mrs. Borwick began the day with the Lord's Prayer and then on to news. Everyone tried to get in the latest gossip from the community, as well as the world news.

After this our shiny spelling books would keep us busy learning new words - like write and rignt, which seemed so frustrating that they would sound the same, yet look different! If we were correct in our spelling we would get a gold star. Next came everyone's favorite (not really), math! We never had to stay at our desks all the time though, many times we would have "flash card" sessions in the stairwell or outside if it was nice After all this heavy brain work, we would rush into a 15 - 20 minute recess. We had so many choices of things to do in that great play yard, it was always a group concensus which decided the outcome! In the fall we played Baseball, Kick the Can, Dodgeball, or Hide and Seek. Winter-time fun in the snow was always great, despite the cold, "Fox and Geese" trails would cover everywhere. Snow forts for snowball fights would give the greatest protection from the "other guys". In the spring we would play Hop-Scotch and mar-bles, and dump trucks on the dry ground on the south side of the school. Even though that part was dry we somehow managed to track mud into the school, much to Mrs. Borwick's displeasure! By late spring and summer it was baseball, and more baseball! It was funny how we had all the fancy swings and slides and monkey bars - and yet their use never matched our creative minds. When the trees were there we would have great fun playing make believe in the maze of caraganas and poplars. The guys played war, while the girls played with their dolls, all in secret places in

John Moar, Randy McGhee, Clinton Moar, Maureen Moar, Stacy McGhee 1965   Todd McGhee

those trees. Our greatest sadness came when the scrapers came and got rid of those wonderful secret places in the trees - to make the road visibility safer. (I still think it was a mistake).

After recess we finished our math and moved on to Social Studies. We would take on great projects like 3-D dough maps, reports and presentations about Alberta, Canada, and the world. By 12 o'clock though, our stomachs told us it was time to eat.

Orkney School Students   1973 Many modern conveniences.

The lunch hour was great! No one was-ted time eating so as to get in every last minute of play. Indoors or out, we still had fun. During miserable weather, that seemingly small building gave us a world of play to explore. "Hide and Seek," "I spy with my little eye," and "Prisoners Base" would keep us occupied in the basement. When we were really bored we would play cards, snakes and ladders or crokinole. By 1 o'clock the ringing of the bell cal-led us back. After roll-call Mrs. Bor-wick always took 15 minutes to read a chap-ter or two from a novel. By the time ev-eryone would get really interested, she would stop, leaving us in suspense until the next day. It was now reading time and for an hour and a half we would explore the English language until we had verbs and adjectives coming out of our ears. The last recess came right after, leav-ing us an hour from 2:30 to 3:30 for the daily specials. This part of the day was always different. Mondays were Science, Tusdays - Health, Wednesdays - Recreation,

40
Thursdays - Music and Fridays (everyone's favorite) Art. Our science classes were a good example of Orkney - we did not have much fancy equipment but we did have all the necessary times for most experiments. In music we did a lot of singing to records and following in our home-made song books. Then in Art the creative hands of all were busy, finger painting or carving plaster of paris.

The school year wouldn't be complete without mentioning the excitement of Halloween and Valentine's Day. But the favorite school function was the Christmas concert. It was usually held the last Friday before school was out in December, we would assemble to recite poems, sing songs and act in plays. We would spend months in practise, all for one night of butterflies! The excitement would build until Santa appeared and gifts were exchanged. It was always a mystery how he would find our little school from such a long way.

The school year always concluded with the School Sports Day. Races, baseball, prizes and awards and candy at the booth added to the excitement of the start of the summer vacation. From this day, the grade sixers moved on to bigger and better things - for myself, the next six years were at Three Hills School.

Students watching Educational T.V. at the Orkney School 1973

It was sad that after many years - in the summer of 1975 the school closed. Many knew it had to ultimately happen - lack of students in the community. Nowadays local children are bussed 25 miles to Three Hills. I remember how the Three Hills School Board tried to close the school before, and how the local

The newly built Orkney School, 1929

To keep up with the changing times many modern conveniences such as: power running water, natural gas furnace, telephone and television were added.

To keep the students on par with other students in larger schools, new books, modern science, art and music supplies, duplicating equipment, many library books and new desks were added. This kept the school functioning as well as any other school in Alberta.

people had fought hard to keep it open. The board felt we were getting an inferior education as well as it was too expensive to operate. I never felt we had a poor education there and many have gone to succeed in many endeavors. In a time when many want to return to the basics of learning, smaller pupil - teacher ratio, less structural schedules for more individual learning, it is clear that Orkney offered all that and more. It used to be that a one-room school education was for the less fortunate, today it is a desired option in many areas. We think we only have memories but I think we gained something rare and invaluable. I feel very proud to have been part of this local tradition, something that now is a legacy of our past.

4-H was a huge part of growing up. First we were involved in the Dinosaur Sheep club, then moved in to the Hesketh-Orkney 4-H beef club. Eight years of raising a Hereford calf, learning all sorts of skills with animals as well as book keeping and of course Public Speaking. Show and sale days were always the end to the year, and although I never took home any prizes for my calf, I did quite well with other aspects of 4-H, lessons learned for life. For me, attending Club week and other 4-H group and club activities like Hi-way clean up, community and district events gave me confidence in myself to take on most any life challenge.

I so enjoyed farming, driving the tractor, grain truck, combine, sprayer. Whatever needed to be done, Dad would teach us, and when we goofed up (like catching the harrows on a fence post or getting the tractor stuck in the slough), we knew we would catch hell, but it would never happen again.

I was always good with my hands. I could not have had a better teacher than my father. Following in his footsteps, I learned all aspects of farming, as well as wood working and electrical skills. Dad and I spent several hours together on all sorts of projects. We did several renovations, both for us and neighbours, from the rumpus room to new bathroom cabinets. We did it all, and the lessons learned I took with me for life.

My mom and grandma were also very important teachers. Because I had two brothers, my mom was not going to let any job be "woman's work." We all learned how to cook, clean, do laundry and, of course, help with the garden and yard work. Helping Grandma was extra-special, as sometimes she would pay us cash or take us to town for a treat.

I will forever cherish memories of shelling peas and pulling weeds, sitting around playing crib, and family dinners.

Involvement in the community was also important in growing up. There was always something going on at the school, from Halloween to Christmas concerts, and Valentine parties, monthly socials and dances, to the summer Sports Day. During the summer on Wednesday nights there was pick-up soft ball. Gathering at the river for swimming and bonfires was a summer Saturday tradition. Ice skating on the dugout filled many winter days.

Sundays, we attended church and Sunday school at the Orkney Presbyterian church. Most of the neighbours would be there, taking time to thank God for all the blessings He had given this group of people. After church, lunch parties moved every week from one house to another. The little things we did always kept that sense of community and the importance of sharing.

The time came to leave the one-room schoolhouse. The bus ride was over an hour to Three Hills School. Grade 7 had its challenges; for the first six years I only had one classmate, and now I had twenty-six. The structure of homeroom and moving between timetabled classes was a shock that I had to adjust to. We caught the bus at seven a.m. and got home at five p.m. I transferred to Drumheller Composite High School in Grade 10. Here, instead of academics I could take carpentry, drafting, and work on skills that interested me. I graduated in 1981 with an Alberta diploma, and right away got a job in the construction industry, continuing to help on the farm when I could.

In February of 1981 I took a holiday in Florida, and it was there I met my future wife. We were married in June, 1983. Joan and I bought a house in Drumheller as I began a new job as carpenter at the Royal Tyrell Museum. During my time there, I was able to earn my journeymen carpentry ticket. Being part of the interior construction crew was a dream job that I will never forget, nor the people I worked with. I felt such a sense of pride on opening day, September 25th, 1985.

My next significant life event was the birth of my son, Bradley, in 1987, and then my daughter, Alyse, in 1989. As a man with a young family and a career in the building industry, life was busy. Home life and family life were challenges to balance. We were now living on the family farm, in the original farm house. The kids were in school, and both my wife and I were working. We kept busy with school activities, and were active in the Knox United Church in Drumheller. Being on the road between the farm, Three Hills and Drumheller was taking its toll on all of us, so we bought a house in Drumheller so that we could spend more time together as a family.

My son was in Scouts, and I was as a Scout Leader. My daughter and her mother were involved in Girl Guides. The kids were both involved in the Morrin Multi 4-H club. Alyse was in sewing classes and Bradley in small motor instruction. As I look back, I wonder how we did all that--run our business, belong to the Chamber of Commerce, Canadian Badlands Passion Play, the Drumheller Ski Hill, church and family. Somehow, it all worked.

McGhee Family 1996

With the kids graduating from school and moving on to college, change was difficult. As a couple we had grown apart, and working through the process of separation was painful. We worked hard with counselling as to how best move forward.

For me, it was a time of lots of soul searching. As a man in his mid-forties, my life seemed to be coming apart. Work was super-busy with lots of changes, and I found that I was not as happy with what I had been doing as before. For years, I had put my family and friends first, and in that process I had lost a lot of my self-esteem. A good friend of mine in Red Deer suggested that I take a personal development course, and I did. I came to realize where I was in life, and that it was time for change. Depression in men is very common and not really talked about. So many men in their forties tend to turn to booze and drugs to help them through. I was lucky not to go down that road. I sought mental health advice from my doctor, and with medication and counselling I got back on track.

The personal development course was a huge part of the process of change. The intensive five-day course took me to the deepest parts of my soul, helped me to understand who I was, and gave me the courage to take control of my life. With help from the facilitator and the other participants, I left the course with a totally new outlook on life, and supportive people who were there to walk with me. As new people appeared in my life, I was better able to handle stress and I found new ways to cope with things. I was so much more aware of how I interacted with my surroundings, my work and family life, that I felt healthier, happier and more excited about new opportunities being presented to me. I was more open to letting God and the Universe help . Changes and challenges became positive, instead of negative events.

Thinking now about soul-searching and learning from difficult times, I remember that several years back I previously I spoke about an experience that my wife and I shared when she was eight months pregnant with our first child. A simple visit to the doctor changed everything, and the hospital called to say I needed to be present for a consultation. I did not know what to expect, so I was both excited and nervous. After meetings with the doctors and several tests, we were told that our baby had died.

My wife would be induced to bring on the birth. This news was so heartbreaking that I cannot express how we were feeling. We had a baby girl who had never taken her first breath, and we now had to plan for her funeral. The kind support from family and friends was overwhelming, however, and helped us move through our grief.

When I spoke about this experience at our home church in Drumheller, the lesson that rang true from my heart was that God helps us through these times, and He gives us the tools and the people we need. If we choose to accept this help and take away lessons both good and bad, happy and sad, we will become stronger people.

As I am a carpenter, I also noted that to make a project go easier or faster there is a wide range of tools to choose from. Some work better than others. The choice of tools is ours.

Sometimes we make a choice that at the time seems wrong. If you look at it from a different perspective and find a lesson in it, you can turn it into a positive. You won't make the same mistake a second time, and if you do, you'll know what tools to use to help you through. Even today, as I think back on all the things in life that I've had to deal with, I'm a better man for learning lessons and moving on. To figure out how to achieve the best outcome every day, and enjoy what life puts in front of me, is a positive kind of challenge.

To best take charge of your life, choose first to be kind to yourself and others. Life is too short not to be happy, and with happiness comes the personal success and prosperity that only you can define.

CHAPTER 1
2010

THE ADVENTURE BEGINS . . .

It was Tuesday, May 19th , 2009. A fantastic morning. To be honest, I find this to be the best part of the day. When I arrived at work, it seemed like most others. As a salesman for a building supply company, my job was to go out, meet new customers, and find out how we could assist them in their project. I was to head west of Red Deer, to a place west of the "Stauffer corner," wherever that was.

The customer had given me directions to their home address: head west on Highway 11, then just after the David Thompson school, turn left on Highway 761 and go south about 16 km. From there, turn right and drive about three kilometers to the stop sign. Turn left, and after half a kilometer, turn right into the driveway with the sign "Welcome to the Lazy M Ranch." Cross the cattle guard and drive into the main yard. Okay, this is easy, I thought, and off I went as usual, as for any other sales call. I had no idea how life-changing this drive would be.

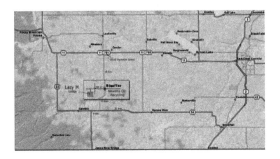

Location of The Lazy M Lodge

As I drove into the yard, I was met by Margie and Lane Moore. They had established an eight-bedroom lodge and ranch where guests were treated to western cowboy lifestyle: wide open spaces, horses, wonderful hospitality, and great food.

As with most clients, there were questions about their prospective project. They wanted to build a new retirement home, providing they could sell their guest ranch. As the afternoon faded away, conversation wandered from the plans for their new house to other topics. I felt unexpectedly comfortable telling them my life story and listening to theirs. We had similar interests and lots in common.

Sitting on the deck with a cold iced tea, looking at the amazing view and watching the water of the North Raven River pass below us, was a very surreal moment. This was the kind of place I had dreamed about all my life. Ever since I was little, I had wanted to run a guest or a fishing lodge. I always thought it might happen in the vicinity of where I grew up, but I was feeling more inclined to new experiences and opportunities. The personal development course had given me a new drive and another perspective on my life. I knew in my heart that this was part of a plan that was laid out for me. Perhaps this was the time to not be afraid, and to take a risk.

As the conversation got back to the new home, Lane pointed out that in order to build it, the guest ranch business would have to be sold. Okay, now I started thinking about the possibilities. Could I buy the ranch, or at least a share of a new venture?

As I drove back to the office in Red Deer, I was aware that this sales call destined; however, I was going through a divorce, I had two kids in college, and money was more than tight. I had to regroup my thoughts and look at all possibilities.

Once I got home that night, I called Marcel. He and I had been friends ever since I had done renovations in his home in Calgary, years before. His opinion and feedback were very important to me. He had always been the perfect sounding board for my crazy ideas, and he had no trouble telling me whether I was on my game or whether I had finally lost it. I told him at length about the Lazy M Ranch, and to my surprise he was very interested in what I had to say. He, too, was at the point in his life and career where perhaps a change was needed. For him to leave a well-paying job he'd had for over thirty years, however, might be a hard sell. There had to be a hook that I could offer him.

The following Monday, I returned to the Moores' to review the quote and to go over plans and pricing for their new home. The conversation soon changed from the housebuilding project to how interested I might be at possibly purchasing the Lazy M. I told Margie and Lane I could not do this on my own, that I had talked to a good friend, Marcel, and that he had shown a some interest in what they had built over twenty years. With that, Margie and Lane invited both of us out the next weekend to have the Lazy M experience.

Marcel picked me up Saturday morning, and off we went. Driving down the gravel road into the yard, we both felt a huge weight being lifted from us, and a calm came over us.

The sign at the gateway to the Lazy M

Margie greeted us. She suggested we all go for a walk so that she and Lane could get to know us better. We both felt like little kids and could hardly wait to see the entire place.

Lane was doing work with some horses in the barn. Now, this was not just any barn. Built eight years previously, it was forty by eighty feet, with an office and tack room. Upstairs, there was a fully-contained one-bedroom suite for staff, complete with a kitchen, living room and a beautiful deck that overlooked the North Raven River.

Lane asked what we would do with the barn if we bought the Lazy M. Were we horse people, and would we take over the trail riding part of their business? That was how they had become successful. We had not really set anything in stone as far as what we would do with the barn, but we both felt our plan would be to perhaps re-purpose it into a hall.

Margie took us down the property to where they had direct access to the North Raven River. What an amazing spot! There was a little bridge over the crystal clear water. I had always dreamed that my retirement place would be alongside a river.

We walked back up to the main yard and Margie took us into the fishermen's cabin. This had been their original home, and you could feel the love and charm that they had built into it. It was no cabin--it was an eighteen hundred square foot residence that had four bedrooms, two bathrooms, laundry room, and a huge living room. Again, Marcel and I were blown away, thinking of all the possibilities.

First view of the Lodge and fishermen's cabin

As we walked up the wooden sidewalk to tour the main house, there was a feeling of comfort and a sense of being home. Walking onto the veranda, the view was breathtaking. The North Raven River was just below and the mountains could be seen to the west. The main entry was warm with wood finished walls and floors. The kitchen was to the right, and featured a table almost 20 feet long in front of the main dining room. The exchange of stories, the smell of food cooking, and a beautifully-set table, made this place feel alive and inviting, and something that we wanted to be a part of. Margie and Lane were making sure we got the message.

Entrance way to the Lodge

Dining room

Kitchen

Sunroom

Main floor bedroom

Main area upstairs

TV Room

Upstairs bedroom

Aerial photo of the Lazy M , 2010

As we explored, we came to the sun room, with a wood stove and priceless views facing south and west. Margie showed us the back deck with a hot tub, three full main-floor guest suites, and two washrooms with showers. Each room was so cozy, with wood accents and custom-made bed comforters. On the second floor there were five rooms. Four were guestrooms, and one was an office. There was also a TV room, again with amazing views to the west.

Margie invited us to sit on the deck, where she brought us a cold beer while we waited for Lane to come up from the barn. She went into the kitchen to start to prepare supper. Both Marcel and I were still in a state of excitement and apprehension when Lane came along. He was curious about what we were thinking of the Lazy M, and he began to tell us stories about running the guest ranch in the past. An amazing storyteller, he had Marcel and I laughing and crying about their experiences. He told us about guests from all over the world. We were taken by how everyone was treated as family, and how many guests returned often to visit.

At supper, Lane sat at the head of the big table, Margie to his left, and Marcel and I sat across from them. As with most meals at the Lazy M, there was lots of food and conversation. We sat there for hours, talking back and forth, learning about each other. We moved out on the deck after supper to share a glass of wine and watch the sunset.

Before long, we decided it was time for bed. Margie and Lane walked us over to the fishermen's cabin where they had prepared two rooms for us for the night. We felt so cozy there, and had all the comforts of home. Marcel and I talked for hours about what we had experienced, and what we might expect if we headed off on this new journey.

Breakfast was at 8 o'clock, "and don't be late!" said Lane. Going back to the main house, the smell of fresh coffee, bacon, and pancakes was the start to a great morning. Lane and Margie were quite excited to hear our feedback about their business and whether we thought it was something we would like to consider.

It was time to talk numbers and timelines. Now, Lane is the type of man who tells it like it is--no beating around the bush with him! Lane and Margie made it very clear that this was their baby, and after almost twenty years, letting it go would be hard. The thing was, as their new house would be less than a quarter of a kilometre away, the next owners would also be their closest neighbours. They were looking for new owners who would take good care of the place and continue to build on what they had started, be that a horseback riding ranch or some other form of country retreat,

Both Marcel and I had grown up as farm kids. We knew all about rural living. With our combined skills--my carpentry, maintenance, handyman and people skills and Marcel's strong background in business management, computer skills, and his passion for cooking and looking after people, we would be a good combination to take over from Lane and Margie, who were also getting excited.

After the wonderful weekend we had to leave, and start to consider what the future might hold for us. Marcel had been at his job for more than thirty years. He had a staff of 180 people, solid business relationships, and of course ties to the Calgary city lifestyle. I had worked in construction almost twenty-five years, had more than fifty co-workers and a long list of customers.

A key factor in our decision-making was that this new venture could mean it would be possible for just the two of us to run it, without employees. This alone helped with our decision process. Our next task would be to weigh all the options and make this potentially life-changing decision.

On Tuesday, a hiccup developed. Margie called to tell us there was another group interested in buying the Lazy M Ranch. This group had made an offer, subject to several conditions, and Margie and Lane had decided to have a good look at it. As you can imagine, Marcel and I were disappointed and sort of broken-hearted, but before our conversation ended, Margie and Lane had a suggestion. The group that was looking to purchase would need a business manager and a maintenance man. They knew after our visit with them that we would be a perfect fit. If we were interested they would pass our names along to this possible buyer .

A part of us wanted to do this on our own, but again, at this time in lives we were open to what the Universe was presenting to us. The day after, we received a call from Kath, who was spearheading the possible purchase of the Lazy M Ranch. Marcel came up from Calgary and we met with her and her group in Red Deer. Everyone was happy with how their business plan could work very well with our own objectives.

The next hurdle was to meet with the County Council to discuss the process of rezoning and future development. Let's just say that unfortunately for the other group, this process became the turning point in the plans. With new regulations and a long list of "not in my backyard" opponents, the process for them to purchase the Lazy M was going to be long and difficult. Kath and her group decided to rescind their offer and seek other ventures.

As I have said, there comes a time when the Universe shows you what it has in store, and now the ball was back in our court. It was now or never, so Marcel and I began the process of putting together a strong business plan and coming up with the cash to make a formal offer. We spent days going over the numbers, not only the purchase price, but also the cash for redevelopment, advertising, and a growing list of other things.

With our backgrounds, training, and individual strengths, Marcel and I we were able to put together a solid plan and make the offer. By the end of July, we were committed and ready to present a business plan and formalize our offer. As of September 30, 2009, I would give notice to the company I was working for in Red Deer, and move into the fishermen's cabin, which would be our full-time residence. Marcel was listing his home in Calgary, and would continue to work until December 31. Our official takeover date would be January 15th , 2010.

When you make a life-changing decision like this, there are lots of things to organize. Both Marcel and I were just entering our fifties, so it was time to clean house, de-clutter and make a fresh start. We both had lots of other things to consider as well. The first order of business was to tell our kids what we were up to. I met with my son, Brad, and daughter, Alyse, and explained to them that Marcel and I were going to take on a new joint venture. They were in their early twenties, and their understanding of change was that it was really no big deal. They said, "Dad, we will be behind you."

Having their support, I felt confident to move on.

Marcel's kids, Michelle and Shaun, were also very supportive, and said, "Dad you're old enough to make your own decisions." With that behind us, it was time to let our co-workers and other family members know our plans. A few people said, "Good for you guys!" and others, "Are you two freaking nuts?!"

Marcel's home sold within days. His workplace was somewhat surprised when he announced he was quitting his job to buy and operate a guest lodge out by Caroline, Alberta. He was asked to stay on in an advisory position for the next few months.

Both of us were leaving really good jobs and incomes to start a new venture, with potentially very little revenue to start, living 'way out in the country. This was an exciting challenge, however, and we felt very confident of our future success.

So, as Christmas 2009 and the New Year approached, there were several things that needed to get done. It was important to make sure that this would be our refuge after the working day.

I had moved into the fishermen's cabin in mid-October and began some kitchen renovations, adding a pantry and new countertops. The two back bedrooms were also renovated to include larger closets, new lighting, and fresh paint. I created a small lobby where guests would register, and a new office space for all our bookwork. The living room and dining area were painted and the layouts rearranged to work better for Marcel's furniture.

January 15, 2010 was a sunny day. Until then, it had been very cold. The sunshine and the warming temperatures encouraged us in our new life venture. The next few days were spent organizing furniture and getting used to our new lifestyle. Our goal was to make the Lodge a comfortable and inviting space for guests to feel right at home, a place to rest, relax, and recharge.

Our business plan included building a new website, seeking out new advertising. direct mail-outs, and attending trade shows. As we were not going to carry on with horseback riding and the mountain trail rides, there was some business carry-over from Margie and Lane. Our shift in the business would include a new format, more geared to retreats, personal getaways, family reunions and weddings.

The phone was not exactly ringing off the wall and email inquirers were very slow, but for the most part we expected that. You expect challenges when you change jobs, let alone careers and a lifestyle, and we were ready to hang in there for a couple of years to set the new direction for the Lazy M Lodge. We were just happy to be able to make this place our new home.

The first guests to write in our guest book were good friends who came from Calgary. It was February 14th, Valentine's weekend, and it would be a good test run. Brenda and Zach were a great support in encouraging us to move, and they were excited to see what the Lazy M Lodge would be like. Our other friend, Val, was also instrumental in supporting what we were hoping to accomplish here. It was awesome to welcome them. To say the least, they were over-the-moon with how beautiful, comfortable, and homey the Lodge was.

The next test was our cooking. The dinner menu was barbecued steak and all the fixings, including dessert. To be able to sit down and share our home cooking along with a good glass of wine was a great way to begin our business.

"Absolutely amazing, beautiful, peaceful and refreshing. I absolutely love it! Good luck guys," Val

"Doing nothing is just what we love to do. Love the peace, serenity, and hospitality. Can't wait to come back!" Brenda and Zach

Okay, the waters had been tested and we needed to make a few adjustments, get in the groove of cooking, cleaning, and becoming a place that people would look forward to returning to visit. Bobby in Edmonton phoned, looking for a space that could accommodate twelve people for a four-day retreat.

"Of course, we can help you. When are you thinking of doing this?" His reply was the following week, February 25-28. That was only ten days away. Okay, no problem, we can handle this! This was our first group booking and we had a lot to do to get ready. We had to plan menus for breakfast, lunch, and dinner, plus snacks for break times, and we had to set up meeting rooms. We made our first big shopping trip to Red Deer, with a long list of supplies and groceries.

We had some anxieties. It was hard to believe that we had $1000 worth of food and supplies for this group. Would that be enough? What if someone doesn't like our cooking? How would we deal with a special dietary requirement? From growing up on the farm, we had learned to plan ahead and have lots of backup plans. We were going to have to rely on our gut feelings and just do our best.

The morning of February 25th came. Here we go! We greeted the guests as they arrived, making new friends, and got them all comfortable in their rooms. We had set the loft in the barn to be used as a meeting space. Supper was to be at five o'clock.

As everyone came from the hall and began to sit around the table, we started serving the food. They seemed to be extremely hungry. There was not too much conversation and every-one seemed shy; no one even talked about their experience, or how their day was going. We were hoping we had not said anything wrong, or that they weren't enjoying the meal. Now, every plate and bowl was cleaned out, there was hardly a crumb left, so obviously they enjoyed the food, but no one even said "thank-you" as they finished up their supper, which seemed odd to us.

As the group gathered and went back to the hall, Bobby the facilitator took us aside and said, "Guys, that supper was awesome. The group really enjoyed it. One thing I forgot to mention is that this is a silent retreat and mealtime is a time for reflection. Rest assured no one had any problem with you or the food, and the facility is great."

That explained a lot, so we were on the right track. It would not be until Sunday that the guests would be able to talk to us. Over the next few days, we got used to the fact that the group was relaxing, enjoying their course and appreciating our food, accommodations, and our level of service. They began to give us the thumbs up.

On Sunday we were invited to join the group for lunch. There was much talk about what a wonderful place, outstanding food, and over-the-top hospitality we had given them the past few days. Their sincerity very touching to hear, and their praise was what we had hoped to achieve. As they packed their bags for home. We were told we had a special place and a gift for looking after people.

As Bobby was getting ready to leave, he took the time to share the participants' appreciation with us. "In all my years of running this course, I have never experienced such great energy. Not just your facility, but also the food. You two gracious hosts took such great care of us. You should be proud of your new venture. It offers challenges, but your hearts and souls are meant to be here. I wish you nothing but success."

Wow! It was so encouraging for us to get such positive feedback, and actually kind of hard to accept. This was the first moment of validation, proof that perhaps we were destined to be here at this place and time.

The phone and email enquiries were starting to come in, and our plans for making the Lazy M Lodge more ours were beginning to take shape. As we moved into March and April, the snow began to melt away and people began to venture out to our area to visit us. Steve and Amber from Camrose chose the Lazy M Lodge for a couple's getaway weekend.

"What a great place, awesome scenery, great food, peace and quiet, and awesome hosts. Can't wait to come back. It was our perfect weekend getaway."

With the snow all gone, it was project time. Our good friend Eric came up from Calgary to give us a hand. We would increase the size of the back deck adjacent to the hot tub. It had to be large enough for twenty guests to gather around a fire pit. We also wanted to widen the sidewalk to the front entrance and to build a large sloped sidewalk, for easier access to the lodge. We also built a new barbeque space just off the kitchen. This gave the lodge some new features to enhance the guests' experience .

Eric and back deck construction

New front deck and walk way

Easter Sunday, April 4th , was a time for family to gather. I was happy to have my mom and dad, brother Todd his wife Faye, their two children Keara and Delaney, along with my two kids Bradley and Alyse for Easter dinner. This was everyone's first visit to the Lazy M Lodge to see what Randy and Marcel were building. For me, it was important to get approval and support from my family, as over the past few years there had been several changes in jobs and relationships that had caused some stress.

My dad was not in good health, so this trip from Drumheller to Caroline and an overnight stay was a big deal for him. It was a warm spring weekend and after everyone arrived and got settled, we gave them the grand tour. Everyone was very impressed with the Lodge and the beauty that surrounded it. My dad knew that with my background, this place would only just get better. As I heard myself tell them about the plans to turn the barn into a hall it seemed ambitious. but very doable.

We shared lots of laughs that weekend and I could feel the support for me and Marcel in this new business. Remembering my dad telling me that I had finally found the place I was meant to be brings tears to my eyes. It was the only time my dad would see this place and be able to spend time here. It was truly a blessing for our families and a great reassurance that what we were doing would be successful.

Every morning Marcel and I would get up and do a walk around the property. Quite often this involved meeting Pete the porcupine. Pete had established a den just down from the main lodge and in his routine was to walk across the deck every morning down the steps and wait for the melon rinds to be thrown out after breakfast. It was quite a sight to see Pete holding one with his front paws and enjoying it.

Pete the Porcupine

Even though he was an old porcupine it was amazing how fast he could run. One particular morning, Marcel was going out of the house and thought he saw something in the flower beds. Thinking it was a cat he ventured closer. To his surprise, and also to Pete the porcupine's, there was a quick exit of both parties in opposite directions. Marcel knew next time to keep a bit more distance from Pete.

One morning when we got up, we noticed that Pete was still sitting in the grass where we had fed him the day before. There seemed to be little movement and we were concerned that something was wrong. So, with a long pole we kind of poked at Pete, only to have him fall over as he must have died the night before. Now, he was a big guy and it was no easy task to pick him up off the lawn and then proceed to dig a hole behind the barn and bury him..

Our next booking was from the Safe Harbour folks out of Red Deer. This was the group that had been interested in purchasing the Lazy M Ranch. They were very encouraging and happy that Marcel and I had taken over this venture. Our relationship with them was to grow in the coming years. They were pleased with the changes we had made and were very impressed by what good cooks we were. Their meetings went very well, and they enjoyed being able to gather on the back deck on a nice sunny day, taking advantage of the peace and quiet that leads to a very productive weekend.

May began with Scott and his group from Red Deer College. A three-day workshop for twelve was such a pleasure, and was the beginning of several more gatherings for them here at the Lazy M Lodge.

"I leave full of hope and I am re-energized. This beautiful place is the reason. Thank you both. PS: The food was awesome." Scott

Marcel's family were getting the itch to see what he was up to. His daughter Michelle and Matt, as well as his son Shaun, had spent time with us and were happy to see the awesome transformation in their dad. He was so much more relaxed and happier. His sister Sylvianne made a trip down from Peace River to see what the Lazy M was all about and to give her brother some cooking and baking tips. She could not get over the fact that Marcel would take such a risk, but was so proud of him and his new outlook on life.

Sylvianne taught us her method of baking buns and bread. For her, this was easy; for us, not so much. We watched her very carefully, made several notes, and when we thought we had everything figured out, it was our turn to give it a try. Well, let's just say we created bread that was inedible but could be used for footballs. It would take us some time and practice to get this baking thing down pat.

The next visitors were Marcel's brother, Ray, and his wife Julie from Peace River. Their daughter Nikki joined us from Calgary on the May long weekend. We were also able to relax and tour the area to see what else was close by. We enjoyed a beautiful day golfing at the Caroline and District golf course, and toured many a back road to see what this part of Alberta offered. It was great to enjoy dinner and drinks on the veranda overlooking the North Raven River. Marcel's brother was very impressed with this new venture. He was excited that they would have a new place to visit, too.

As the month of June began, we were happy to host Bobby and "The Wall" program with participants from Edmonton. We were much more prepared for his group this time, and we so enjoyed having them experience the energy of the Lazy M Lodge.

"Thanks for providing a beautiful, peaceful place for our retreat. The food was great and we wish you much luck and success. I will be back." Al S.

On a beautiful Friday afternoon in June, our next group of guests would also be from Edmonton--The Fishin' Hole, for their annual fly fishing school. Now, as this was their twelfth year booking the Lazy M, this was going to be a test for us. They were accustomed to being treated in a certain way. We were concerned about how they would find the accommodations and the food under our new ownership, and we were determined to meet and exceed their expectations.

There were two managers from Edmonton, Brian and Mike, and Bill from Calgary. As Marcel and I welcomed them back to the new Lazy M Lodge, they were quite surprised to see the changes already made. As we set the table for supper, they were delighted that we were serving them a barbecued salmon dinner, rice, steamed vegetables, spinach salad, and strawberry rhubarb pie for dessert. With the first meal done and all cleaned up, we asked for their feedback. All agreed they were impressed with the changes, and that the food was exceptional.

This particular weekend we were delighted to have a new employee start his tenure at the Lazy M Lodge--a Scotch Collie puppy, like Lassie.

I had never had a dog as a puppy. Growing up on the farm, we always had dogs that were rescues and needed good homes We had gone down on the Saturday morning to meet the breeder and check out his last Collie pup. Upon arriving, the owner whistled over the mother dog and behind her was an amazing eight-week-old male. Marcel and I instantly fell for this little fella. Bringing him home to the Lazy M Lodge was going to change things a lot. It would take time for us to train him properly and make sure that he would grow up knowing it was his home.

He was a real hit with the guests and he bonded not only to us, but to everyone that he met. At dinner that night, several names were tossed around for this new employee at the Lazy M. Somehow the name Rusty seem to fit his demeanour, and so began his life with us.

Rusty, our new puppy

Well, we did it! The managers and participants of The Fishin' Hole had a great weekend. They so enjoyed the facility and the meals that we took the next booking for their July fly fishing school right away.

"The new Lazy M is perfect. Thanks, guys. Can't wait to come back." Bill from Calgary.

"It's so great to get to know the new owners of the Lazy M. Thank-you for your hospitality. The food is great. You have made our fly fishing weekend a great success." Brian, Edmonton.

The next weekend in June, we welcomed a new group of people who came to get away from the city and enjoy some of the country life and fresh air. For years they had been having their meetings and getaways at a small lake, where they had to bring their own food, their own bedding, and plenty of mosquito spray, but it was becoming too hard to organize. They were attracted by the fact that we offered an all-inclusive format, real beds, private rooms, and an outdoor hot tub. For them it was for them a real upgrade. They were also very happy that we had camping spots available. They so enjoyed the privacy and the wide-open spaces that several people wanted to come back in the fall.

"Marcel and Randy, you are amazing hosts. Your hospitality and amazing cooking skills have made this a great getaway. I just love this place. It is a real gem. I can't wait to come back." Blair

We are finding out how fortunate we are to live here. Becoming good friends with our neighbours Travis and Natascha, Audrey and Dolly, Kate, and of course Margie and Lane, was part of the lifestyle. At the beginning of summer solstice, it was great to share stories and learn about each other on our new back deck.

Before moving out to the Lazy M, I had met some great people in Red Deer. Leonard, Erin, and their family arrived on the June 25th weekend to celebrate their twenty-fifth wedding anniversary. All they wanted was a small personal gathering and we were able to give them just what they wished for--a beautiful supper to celebrate their anniversary. They were more than just guests, they are friends.

As July was in swing, so was the fishing. Several new guests began to book for some fly fishing on the North Raven River and to rest, relax, and recharge. We were excited to have guests from Denver, Colorado, Calgary, High Prairie, Edmonton, and Red Deer. And our friends from The Fishin' Hole were back again for their fly fishing school! This time, they had twelve participants and three instructors, and besides learning how to fly fish, there was lots of laughter and good food.

"What a great weekend! We learned so much, had so much fun, and look forward to coming back to the Lazy M again!" Brian

Little did I know what the next few weeks were going to bring. My dad had been in the Drumheller Hospital for several weeks, and his health was slowly failing. Whenever I could, I drove to Drumheller to spend time with him and the rest of the family. My oldest brother Stacy, his wife Ruth and son Gavin, made their way out from Victoria.

One Sunday, my dad told us all that we needed a break, and to go spend some time up at the Lazy M. At supper on Sunday night, we were all together. Stacy and his family, along with Todd my younger brother, his wife Faye, and daughters Keara and Delaney had a wonderful evening visiting. After a good night's rest, the next morning at breakfast we received a phone call from the hospital that my Dad was failing quickly. As we all loaded our cars and headed back to Drumheller for the two-hour drive, our minds and hearts began to feel a terrible loss. By the time we got to the hospital in Drumheller, my Dad had passed away. He had known that we all needed to be well-rested for what the rest of the week had in store for us. One is never ready when a parent passes away, but you do find strength in family and friends. I was so fortunate to have such a loving and caring group of people around me at that time.

With all the improvements we were making at the Lazy M, one of our guests had recommended that we apply for the Clearwater County beautiful yards competition. We were fortunate that the flower beds and a lot of the grounds were in good shape. We just tuned them up, and were proud when the judges came by to look. We did not win that year, but we were certainly recognized for our hard work.

August proved to be a month of visitors from all over the world. We hosted fishermen from Ontario, Washington DC, the United Kingdom, as well as several local Albertans looking for that new place to fish and take a break.

"This place is unbelievable. A trout stream right out your back door! A great day of fishing well into the night. The food was great, the bed so comfortable. Top notch." Brandon, Centerville Virginia USA

As with any new business, some days were greatly challenging. There are those "what have we done?" moments. For me, life was moving along, but dealing with my Dad's passing had taken more energy from me than I expected.

Marcel, was finding it difficult for other reasons, although we were both enjoying meeting new people and were amazed at the support for us in our new business and adventure. Marcel had to make a big adjustment, however; the day-to-day to challenges of income and expenses were stressful. The past thirty years of being fully-employed and receiving a steady paycheck had made him confident that he could provide for himself and his family without worrying. Being his own boss, paying his own bills, writing his own paycheck was not quite what he thought it was going to be. He had to rely on faith that the business would grow, and be happy living in the country with lots of fresh air, peace and quiet. He decided to drive home to Peace River to see family for a few days, and to figure out if this was the direction his life was supposed to take.

After a couple of days, he returned having decided to get through a few more bookings and then perhaps move back to Calgary and the corporate world.

Our friend Scott from Canmore called and he was going to drive up with a friend to see what the Lazy M was all about. It was a beautiful fall day and Marcel and I were working in the barn, washing walls, cleaning, and getting it ready so that we could renovate it during the winter. When Scott arrived, he introduced us to Leonard, who was from Pine House, Saskatchewan, and here in Alberta looking for a place to do some workshops for the First Nations community. We began by touring Leonard and Scott around the property, showing them what our future hopes and dreams were for the Lazy M. While in the barn, Leonard asked Marcel if they could go speak privately for a few moments. So, the two of them went up to the Lodge and Scott and I continued walking the property and talking about planned changes.

At this time, Marcel was of the mindset that it was time for him to move on. The Lazy M was not in the cards for him, and he intended to share his thoughts with me at the right time. Leonard got right to the point. He told Marcel that the grandfathers had sent him there that day to speak to us and to encourage us in our new business venture. Leonard told Marcel he was surprised that he wanted to leave this place, and this of course caught Marcel off-guard. He had not told anyone yet that he was thinking of moving back to the city. Who was this fellow who seemed to know about his intentions?

Marcel didn't know what to feel about this. Leonard explained that the grandfathers wanted to make sure that we would use this place for many good purposes. Leonard went on to tell Marcel that he needed to rethink this decision to move away from the Lazy M. Creator and the grandfathers were telling him that he had to be patient and follow his dream and long-term plans. This place was where he needed to be. By helping others, he would become a better person. God and the universe had brought him and me here to offer a place of healing to everyone that would come into our lives. Leonard said that these were gifts both Marcel and I had, and essential parts of a whole.

Leonard's insight was so right-on that Marcel's emotions began to come to the surface. Never before had he been so moved. He understood that this decision to serve others at the Lazy M would be life-changing, and his feelings shifted to an even stronger sense of purpose and belonging.

When Marcel and Leonard came out of the lodge, Scott and I were on our way back up for a drink. Leonard said to me that he needed to talk to me, and so we headed off for a walk and a talk. He told me he'd heard that I had been going through many struggles--the loss of my dad, my divorce, the change of employment, and a new career. These were all emotional issues that I'd been hiding from, but I needed to deal with them. I was a little taken aback and had figured Marcel had told him what was going on in my life. Leonard assured me that the grandfathers were speaking through him so that he could guide me and help me to work through some of my problems.

Leonard told me that he was sorry to hear about the loss of my dad, but that my father was proud of me and what I had done with my life. He approved of what I was doing and where I was heading on this journey. He then proceeded to tell me of the conversation he had had with Marcel, and I realized that I had been totally unaware Marcel's plans. I tend to push ahead on a project to avoid dealing with my feelings or worrying about what anyone else might be dealing with. Leonard explained that my energy is so focused on serving others that have lost sight of myself and my own feelings. I needed to sort myself out for the next little while.

Leonard wanted Marcel and me to join them in a healing circle after lunch. Leonard said the energy and need for healing was intense, and to not fear a shift in our energy. To be honest, I was not ready for this, but I felt there was a reason for Leonard's presence, and I was open and to hearing him out. So, we sat in the sunroom. There was lots of happiness, sadness, anger and release.

So, what started out as just another day at the Lazy M turned out to be the beginning of our new sense of purpose Leonard's words had brought us peace. Our path had become clear and we had been given a new sense of support. I would be able to truly grieve my dad's passing, working through all my emotions while finding the balance to help others. Marcel, too, felt his emotions shift and he felt a sense of comfort and renewed energy. We felt reassured that the story of the Lazy M Lodge was to be a blessing, not only for us but for everyone who would experience the energy here. Our connection to this property would allow us to create a place where we and others could truly rest, relax, and recharge.

We are so thankful that God, the Universe, and spirit are with us on this journey

"Words can never express what I have experienced here. There is definitely a strong spirit moving at the Lazy M Lodge, and I would like to encourage others to come and experience this little piece of heaven." Leonard McCallum September 9, 2010

The month of September was turning out to be very interesting. What would come next? Friday, September 17th we were ready for the group known as the "Vegreville Ladies." Their fourteenth year at the Lazy M Lodge was to be the third weekend in September. Fifteen of these ladies were returning to catch up and share some good times. In the past, they had stayed in the fishermen's cabin, gone horseback riding and had had other activities planned for them by Margie, Lane, and their staff. Marcel and I knew this year their visit was going to be different, and we were not sure how it was going to work out.

Upon arrival, the ladies seemed happy to be back and very comfortable with the changes that we had made since their last visit. The real test would come with how well we cooked for them. They were easy to talk to as we prepared supper. They were interested to hear our story, and it was a lot of fun getting to know them over the supper table.

After supper they made their way up to see the former owners, Margie and Lane, and Kate. When they returned about 9 o'clock, they settled in just as they had done in previous years. A phone call from Margie assured us that they liked the new direction of the Lazy M.

"You both surpassed our expectations. For sure, we will be back next September, if not sooner." Caroline

"May your dreams for this place grow to become all and more than you expect. It was a great weekend of friends and food." Ardyth

"Viva the Lazy M, a landmark in my year. Thanks, Marcel and Randy, for allowing the Vegreville Ladies' Book Club and friends to continue our tradition. We look forward to coming back." Janet

The Vegreville Ladies

It was an extremely rewarding weekend for us. Everything went so well and we looked forward to the return of the Vegreville Ladies in the fall of 2011. Both Marcel and I had felt the energy change since Leonard's visit. We suddenly found more joy in what we were doing. We didn't have full bookings, but having a few weekend guests gave us the time and space to learn and improve how we were doing things.

"What can I say? It was like living in a dream for three whole days. Great hospitality, great food, great company, and some great weather. And I can't forget the great views and the great sleeps. Thanks so much for everything, Marcel and Randy. I really enjoy the work you do here at the Lazy M and I am envious of your life. This is the first of many visits." Martin

Our next experience became a memory that warms our hearts. Five lovely women came to see what the Lazy M was all about. They were looking for a special place where they could visit as friends, relax and reconnect. We affectionately call this group of women "the labyrinth ladies," as they enjoyed walking our labyrinth and enjoying the wonderful surroundings. Our Labyrinth was built by the previous owner and her grandaughters. The Rocks were laid out in a pattern which leads you to the center through many twists, turns, wide and narrow parts, much like the path of life. The purpose is to walk and reflect on your path of life. They truly left with a piece of our hearts and they have become such great friends.

The Labyrinth Ladies

"A phenomenally relaxing weekend. What a beautiful location, fantastic accommodations, and great food. I can't wait to come back." Sue, Saskatoon

"I'm sorry to have to leave this wonderful, friendly place. The area around the Lazy M makes it one of the best places to stay. We so enjoyed the friendly hospitality, and your wonderful greeter, Rusty the dog, was great company. See you next year." Marjorie, Edmonton

"Randy and Marcel, I'm so pleased to have shared this place with you. Congratulations on becoming new owners of the Lazy M. I send you many good wishes for your future." Shirley, Saskatoon SK.

"Thank you, thank you! You have such a beautiful spot. Your gracious service, good company, and great food is a complete package! Thank you and good luck with your future plans. I know we will be back again Colleen." Calgary

"Thank-you, Marcel and Randy, for a wonderful weekend. The food in the comfort of the Lodge was beyond great. The scenery is outstanding. We will be back." Lorrie, Edmonton

A different request came from a good friend, Janine. She wanted to bring several ladies out for a farewell supper for a friend heading to Australia. So, in true Canadian/Australian fashion, we did it. There was "shrimp on the BBQ, " and other interesting Australian specialties.

"Thank you for your wonderful hospitality. The detail you went to on the meal was amazing, and the atmosphere that you provided was so much fun. It was a great place to escape to. Thank you!" Shayleen, Cochrane

"U guys rock!" Janine, Red Deer

The meeting with Leonard in September led to a new type of retreat at the Lazy M. Leonard and his friend Brad planned to hold some workshops here with the First Nations and also non-indigenous communities. Under the name White Thunderbird Healing, guests were invited to experience a weekend of fellowship, food, and fun.

Leonard never knows what form the workshop will take until everyone is gathered, and then he feels the group's energy and sees the issues that will need to be addressed. His leadership is very informal, yet very powerful. Working with Leonard and Brad has given me, and Marcel, many personal insights, and we have become aware of the healing energy here at the Lazy M. To share our life stories with others and supporting them in their journeys has been an amazing blessing.

In October, fishermen came to take advantage of the fly fishing in the North Raven River. Greg is one of those regular fishermen. He arrived at eight a.m. and we gladly drove him to a spot downstream so that he could spend the day fishing. Around seven in the evening, he returned with stories and photos of his day. Visits like these let us take the take time to enjoy where we are.

Clive and Kathy are also regular guests. Arriving midweek, they have the place to themselves. Clive spends most of the day fishing and Kathy enjoys reading on the deck or by the woodstove. Our supper conversations go on with stories for hours, like we're old friends catching up.

Greg, our most avid and regular fisherman

As November came upon us, the start of our winter meant buying the snow blower and arranging with the neighbours to help keep the laneway and yard open for guests.

Leonard was back for workshops with members of the O'Chiese and the Sunchild First Nations.

We were unprepared for how well our help was accepted by the Native community in running their programs. The elders invited me and Marcel to participate in a sweat lodge, built with willow branches from along the creek, and covered with blankets and buffalo skins. The elders and six more of us entered it, and once we were all inside the blankets and skins were drawn down and closed and no one was allowed to leave. We listened to an elder say prayers, and offerings were made. They had built a big bonfire outside the lodge and from it they carried in heated rocks. Water from the creek was poured onto the hot rocks, creating steam. The air was heavy, yet very soothing. After twenty minutes we emerged. This was repeated three more times to honour the spirit with new prayers and to bless all those taking part.

When we finished, Marcel and I prepared a traditional buffalo stew and bannock for the celebration feast. One of the elders spoke: "This day and this place is for God's and Creator's special people together, white man and Native. The grandfathers are telling us this is a special place full of peace and goodness, and they are smiling down and filling our hearts with love. We are thankful for Marcel and Randy for allowing us to be here, sharing their land and their food with us. We are all truly blessed."

He then proceeded to smudge the lodge and the grounds, for the grandfathers to watch over all who enter. We felt truly honored to be so included. We are so grateful to be where we are, and thankful for our new friends. We look forward to connecting with more shared experiences.

Framing of the sweat lodge

In December, as winter began to move in on us we again, our "silent retreat" friends from the personal development program, "The Wall" came again from Edmonton. They had found the space ideal for people to grow and heal, and a safe environment for them to so some deep work on "self."

"I felt so cozy. You have a wonderful place, it feels like home. Your food and service were 5 Star. Looking forward to returning." Peter, Edmonton

"You are both so amazing, as always. I'm grateful to the universe for bringing me here to the Lazy M Lodge. I will be back often." Melissa

Christmas at the Lazy M is a special time. We celebrated our first Christmas by hosting a decorating party, inviting several friends to spend the weekend with us and turning the Lazy M Lodge into a beautiful Christmas setting for our visitors. It was so much fun, sharing many laughs, drinking rum and eggnog, and getting into the true Christmas spirit.

That year, my family and I were going to spend the holiday in Victoria. Marcel's family came from Peace River and Calgary to enjoy the Christmas holiday season at the Lodge. What a treat it was for them to all stay together under one roof, and sit together to enjoy a meal around the large dining table.

Our first New Year's Eve at the Lazy M Lodge was spent with a group of friends who enjoy coming to rest, relax, and recharge. There was so much laughter, great table games, wonderful food. Of course, there was the outdoor hot tub, and yes, snow angels in swimsuits. I'm happy to say that this has become an annual event.

As the year ended at the Lazy M Lodge, I felt thankful blessed, and looking so forward to the years ahead.

Our first Christmas at the Lazy M Lodge

LAZY M
BREAKFAST RECIPES

When guests awake at the Lazy M, it is usually to the smell of coffee and bacon.
They come into a beehive of activity in the kitchen. A hearty breakfast gets their
day going. A typical breakfast is scrambled eggs, bacon, pancakes, fresh fruit,
juice, coffee and tea. To add variety, we serve waffles, fried ham, sausages, hash
browns, poached eggs, and French toast. We also like to present house specialties,
like the Lazy Mexican Eggs and other recipes that we're happy to share.

MEXICAN EGGS - THE LAZY M VERSION

12 eggs
12 slices ham
12 tbsp salsa
12 tbsp of shredded cheese
Preheat oven to 350°

Grease a 12 cup muffin tin. Fold ham slices into the bottom of each cup. Place a tablespoon of salsa on top of the ham. Break an egg on top, and sprinkle with a tablespoon of shredded cheese, salt and pepper. Bake for 20 minutes, or until the egg yolks and whites are cooked through. Spoon out each egg cup and place on a plate. Serve with rye toast and fresh fruit.

QUICK AND QUICHE

1 cup crumbled bacon or diced ham
1 cup smoked Gouda cheese, cubed
5 eggs, beaten
1 tsp seasoning salt
2 tsp of melted butter
½ cup flour
1½ cups milk
¼ cup fresh parsley (or dried)

Preheat oven to 350°

Place bacon or ham and Gouda cheese in the bottom of two glass pie plates. Combine the remaining ingredients. Fill each pie plate with half the mixture. Bake for 30 minutes. Top with parsley.

BREAKFAST TIPS

- The best way to cook bacon is to put strips on a cookie sheet and bake at 350° for 40-45 minutes. After 20 minutes drain excess grease. Your bacon will be crispy, flat, and easy to serve.

- When we poach eggs for Eggs Benedict, we use a poaching pan. Simmer for 4-5 minutes for soft-boiled. You can't tell on us for using instant International Hollandaise!

- When making French toast, we beat 10 eggs with 1 ½ of milk and two teaspoons of cinnamon. Coat slices of bread and fry until golden brown. Makes 18 pieces.

- Pancakes are a good way of feeding big groups. After trying several brands of pancake mix we have found a couple that work best. Just ask, and we'll guide you in the right direction.

- Freshness has always been important at the Lazy M, so we make sure to buy fresh fruit and eggs, also fresh sausages, bacon, and ham.

- We serve food in bowls to be passed around. This adds to the Lazy M ambiance and encourages guests to chat amongst themselves.

CHAPTER 2
2011

THE HOLIDAYS WERE OVER AND IT WAS TIME TO TAKE ALL OF THE DECORA-tions down and get back on track for whatever might come our way.

White Thunderbird Healing with Leonard and Brad and some guests from Edmonton, Red Deer, Rocky Mountain House all joined us for a retreat early in the new year..

"So very impressed with this place. It is beautiful and such a great experience. Thank you for your hospitality, success to you always. Many blessings." Doreen

In the middle of January, another group of people from Edmonton braved the cold and snow and made it to the Lazy M. With a facilitator from Seattle, Washington, they made this place their home for five days, finding comfort and peace for individual introspection and to build up their spirits. Here, they could dig deep and to be able to figure out how better to serve themselves and others. We felt honored to support them.

"Thank you for allowing me to have this experience at the Lodge. You are fantastic hosts and your smiles are warm and inviting. I could certainly call this place my new sanctuary and hope to return to have another great experience and great conversations. This is the place where I get to restart my new life." Amy, Edmonton AB.

A local business from Rocky Mountain House choose to substitute their Christmas party with a staff celebration after the busy holiday season.

"We had such a beautiful stay. We absolutely enjoyed every minute of it. The food was great. Lloyd and Carole"

Guest bookings were light in February, when it was still cold and snowy. This gave us time to do some renovations in the barn to make a new gathering place ready for the summer. Our good friend Bill from Drumheller help with the project for a few weeks. Gord, Brad, Curt, Jamie, Brian, and Shaun were other friends who gave Marcel and I a hand to get this project completed.

Outside the soon-to-be Gathering Hall

The change begins.

Re-painting the hall.

East end of the hall.

Framing for washrooms

Fireplace stonework

Nearing the end of the renovation

March was kicked off the following weekend with Leonard and White Thunderbird Healing. It was an important time for participants who experienced great change and healing.

"Thank- you so very much, I appreciate everything you have done to make my stay as comfortable as possible. The lodge is beautiful and I have learned so much in my short stay here. I will recommend any of these weekend workshops to anyone. I know it was truly a blessing to come here. This is like a mini vacation that I have needed and wanted for a long time. I'm so glad that I was able to spend it here. Thanks again." Theresa

Ladies groups seem to need more time to organize a getaway from their everyday lives. In April, Joanna, a bride-to-be was accompanied by her bridesmaids and some friends for a stagette weekend. All we can tell you is that they had lots of laughs and made many memories. . . .

Early in May, the onset of spring brought green to the grass and the time to reconnect with Mother Earth. A group from Saddle Lake came to have Leonard from White Thunderbird Healing lead their retreat. We have found that no matter where you come from, there is an energy here, and especially on Leonard's healing weekends when he helps people reconnect with themselves, with others, and with nature.

"What a great place! You both are wonderful hosts. The weather was lovely, food delicious and the countryside beautiful. Thanks for everything, I will be back." Gail

June brings back the Fishin' Hole fly fishing schools. This particular weekend, the weather was awesome and sixteen guests were able to learn how to tie flies, cast a fly rod, and all the related skills. The weekend was a great success.

"What a fantastic experience! We will certainly spread the word." Lori, Edmonton

"Great atmosphere, great food. Words cannot describe what a wonderful weekend it was. See you soon." AJ

We were very happy again to host another group from the Saddle Lake Nation.

White Thunderbird Healing, group photo

"Thank you from the bottom of my heart for your kindness and hospitality throughout the weekend. May Creator send you and your families and your future guests many blessings." Darlene

"You have an awesome place. I have to say it's been a very unique experience, thank-you." Anne-Marie

As the summer wore on, we were happy to have companies and small businesses join us. To have managers from Edmonton and Calgary meet here with their staff for a weekend of team building has worked extremely well. A space that is comfortable and feels homelike allows people to step away from the usual pressures of work and do constructive strategic planning. A meeting outside on a sunny day makes people so much more productive. With good food, people are nourished well, and that helps, too. People leave the Lazy M nourished in their bellies and their souls.

Relaxing at the Lazy M Lodge.

We had the pleasure of hosting a men's group. Their weekend was a full schedule of meetings and activities. After their first lunch, the facilitator asked them if there should be any changes to the schedule. They symbolically burned the schedule, after deciding as a group that it was more important to take advantage of the Lazy M's motto: rest, relax, and recharge. They got to know their co-workers more as friends. As the facilitator said, it was probably exactly what they needed to do.

When visitors come to the Lazy M, they can never anticipate how their experience will affect them.

"The time I had here was amazing. There are so many words I could use to describe it. I am very grateful that I got to spend it with this group, to laugh, cry, share. I look forward to many new experiences. This has really opened my eyes and my heart. Thanks so much." Chris

When groups make reservations, we never know what to expect. The 27th annual Butz fishing trip was one of those groups. When they arrived, twenty-three family members settled in to the Lazy M Lodge. What started out as a father and sons years ago, was now a father, sons, and grandsons enjoying a weekend together, fishing, eating, drinking, and laughing

"This has been the perfect place for our men's fishing trip. We will be back." Casey

We were happy to host our first wedding in July. Candace and Marty exchanged vows on the front lawn, the perfect place for an outdoor wedding. It was a day full of sunshine shared with many guests.

Candace and Marty's wedding day

The Dreamspeakers workshop brought a new energy to the Lazy M Lodge. For 10 days, film industry professionals coached this group of twenty-five creative young First Nations men and women to write scripts, edit, and act in short films. To watch them find their voices and express their feelings and emotions was truly inspiring. Cooking and cleaning for this many people was both a blessing and a huge learning curve for us.

Dreamspeakers Group

"I really enjoyed my stay here. I have never felt so at peace with myself, especially getting away from the busy hectic life in Edmonton and coming here where it is so beautiful and calming. I will be back, so I'm not saying goodbye to my friends. Randy and Marcel and staff are so kind and generous. You taught me a lot about myself without me knowing it. I hope you enjoy my film, called Transformation. On behalf of the Dreamspeakers, plus the big guys, we want to say thank-you for cooking such great food, helping us with laundry, and supporting us whenever we needed it. We love you guys, and Rusty too." Sincerely, Joseph G.

Several guests throughout the summer were here to fish and relax.

"Thanks for the great stay. We look forward to our next fishing trip your hospitality. The food exceeded all expectations." Brian, Alan, Mark Marshfield, Washington DC, USA"

We were excited to host a special 80th birthday for my Aunt Lois. Several family and friends gathered in the hall to help her celebrate .

Lois's birthday party with family

The first large group in our new hall was going to give us the opportunity to show the neighbours what the Lazy M had become. Seventy-five guests attended the annual Clearwater County Agriculture and Community Services Tour. We are very grateful to the county for their support of rural business and tourism. It was a pleasure to host lunch to our new friends in the county. This kind of exposure helps build community and offers us a chance introduce the Lazy M to locals.

Traditions are important, and when it involves close friends, the Lazy M is a great gathering place.

"The weather was wonderful, as was our weekend of rest and relaxation, and all the 'other stuff' we do at the Lazy M. We so appreciate your hospitality. Once again, thank-you for allowing us girls to continue our tradition of gathering at this wonderful place." The Vegreville Ladies

"Thank-you so much for sharing your great space with us. You have a wonderful welcoming place. We appreciate your attention to detail, and that is what makes our stay here so much fun." Shirley- Saskatoon, Sue- Saskatoon, Lorrie- Edmonton, Marjorie- Edmonton, Colleen- Calgary

"People come into your lives just when you need them to. It helps renew your faith to keep following the path you are on. You honoured us with the care and the love that you put into serving our woman's motivational retreat. Thank you for seeing to our every need, and for offering us such a relaxing, holistic, beautiful, and peaceful environment." Veronica

The change of the season and the fall colours is special here at the Lazy M. When guests arrive, the crispness in the air fills the soul with a different energy.

"Thank you for your warm hospitality. Indeed, you have big dreams to reach, but nothing is unattainable. Blessed are the ones who help and love others. Good luck in your future aspirations." Virginia

Offering a safe and fun place for groups works well here. It was perfect for hosting a Halloween party for a small group of brain-injured adults from a Red Deer group home. They enjoyed a group outing had a wonderful meal, and got into the Halloween spirit.

"Thanks guys for your help in hosting us. Everyone so enjoyed the outing, and your wonderful space was a great change for both staff and our residents. We will be back again." Gord

Bookings in November and December began to fill up with several Christmas parties. We hosted a barn dance in support of the Caroline Medical Clinic. A great time was enjoyed by several local neighbours and over $400.00 was raised.

The hall, ready for Christmas

A roaring fire ready to greet the Christmas party guests

A quiet Christmas with family and close friends, enjoying the warmth of wood burning stoves, playing Christmas music, and of course eating lots of food, was just what we to recharge our batteries.

As the year ended, several friends joined us for a pot luck dinner and we welcomed 2012 with fireworks.

Winter at the Lazy M

Cold and snow

DO YOU KNOW HOW MOST PEOPLE
GET JOBS THEY LOVE?

THEY FIRST LOVED THE JOB THEY HAD,
AND EVERYONE NOTICED.

LAZY M
LUNCH RECIPES

A hearty midday lunch at the Lazy M keeps people content with the "rest, relax, recharge" routine. Here are a few of our more popular lunch recipes.

LAZY TURKEY CORN CHOWDER

1 medium onion, chopped
¼ cup melted butter
2 cups water
2 chicken bouillon cubes
3 cups diced turkey or chicken
1 cup chopped celery
5 medium potatoes, cubed
1 can kernel corn, drained
1 can cream style corn
4 cups milk
salt and pepper to taste

Sauté onion in butter until tender. Add water, bouillon cubes, turkey, celery and potatoes. Cook for 30 minutes or until potatoes are tender. Add corn, milk, salt and pepper to taste. Simmer for an additional 30-60 minutes.

SAUSAGE ROTINI PASTA BAKE

6 cups of rotini pasta
4 hot Italian sausage
1 can tomato paste
1 can diced tomatoes
4 cans tomato sauce
3 cups shredded cheese blend

Preheat oven to 350°

Cook pasta until tender. Cut the Italian sausage into small pieces. Combine in a saucepan with the tomato paste, diced tomatoes, and tomato sauce. Add Italian seasoning and salt and pepper to taste. Mix the sauce with the pasta and pour into two 9 x 13 baking dishes. Cover with shredded cheese and bake for 20-30 minutes. Serve with garlic toast and fresh veggies.

LAZY M CHEESE BISCUITS

2 cups of Flour
1/2 cup of butter, (use a cheese grater as helps mix better in the batter)
4 Teaspoons of baking powder
1 Cup of ice cold water
2 cups of Shredded cheese mix (cheddar and Mozzarella)

Pre heat oven to 400

Take 2 cups of flour and the 4 easpoons of baking powder and mix. Add the 1/2 Cup of grated butter along with one cup of ice cold water and mix. Then add the cheese and mix well till you get a nice dough mix. Use a metal baking pan with a sheet of parchment paper and place about an ice cream scoop of the mix per biscuit . You should get about 18 nice size biscuits. Bake at 400 for 12-15 minutes.

LAZY MAN'S CREAMY BURRITO CASSEROLE

1 lb. ground beef
½ medium yellow onion, chopped
2 tbsp taco seasoning
6 large flour tortillas
1 can re-fried beans
3 cups shredded cheese mix
1 can Cream of Mushroom soup
4 oz. sour cream

Preheat oven to 350°

Brown the ground beef with the onion and drain fat. Stir in the taco seasoning and the re-fried beans. In a separate bowl, mix the sour cream and the soup mix. Spread half in the bottom of a 9 x 13 casserole dish. Tear up three tortilla sheets and place them over the sour cream mixture. Spoon Onto these, spoon half of the meat and bean mixture and a layer of cheese. Repeat the layers, ending with cheese. Bake for 20-30 minutes. Yield: 8 to 10 servings.

CROWD-PLEASING LAZY M TACO SALAD

2 lbs. lean ground beef or turkey
2 tsp taco seasoning mix
1 medium red onion, chopped
1 medium yellow onion, chopped
2 heads iceberg lettuce, chopped
4 roma tomatoes, chopped
2 avocados, peeled and chopped
12 cups nacho chips
1 cup Catalina dressing

Brown the beef or turkey with the chopped yellow onion. Add the 2 tablespoons of taco seasoning mix and let cool. Mix together the chopped lettuce, tomatoes, cheddar cheese, avocados, and red onions. Combine the cooled beef mixture with the vegetable and cheese mixture and toss with the salad dressing. Crush nacho chips and add. Serve immediately, before they go soggy. Serve with extra chips, cheese, sour cream and salsa.

THE LAZY M LEMON PASTA SALAD

4 cups multicoloured fusilli pasta
Put all the following ingredients in a large bowl , mix and set aside
3 green onions, chopped
2 cups chicken broth
1 tsp basil
1 tbsp lemon juice
1 tbsp grated lemon rind
¼ cup grated Parmesan cheese
¼ cup melted butter
Vegetable Mix, add to the boiling water and pasta
3 carrots, julienned
½ green pepper, thinly sliced
½ cup red pepper, thinly sliced
4 cups broccoli
4 cups cauliflower
lemon pepper to taste

Cook the pasta in lots of salted boiling water. When the pasta is almost finished cooking, blanch the vegetables in the water just until slightly soft but not cooked through. Drain the pasta and vegetable mix and rinse with cold water. Add to the large bowl and gently stir all the ingredients together and refridgerate, stirring occasionally. Serve cold We like to add garlic bread and cheese and cold cuts to this meal.

It should feed about 12-15 people

IT'S BEING ALIVE, THAT MAKES YOU RICH.

SO EASY TO FORGET!

CHAPTER 3
2012

THIS WAS THE BEGINNING OF OUR THIRD YEAR AT THE LAZY M LODGE. AS THE new year began, so did our uncertainty of what lay ahead.

January is a time for spring cleaning We clean rooms, organize and also figure out how we are going to build the business by advertising. Our bookings are getting stronger with many repeat customers.

In order to cover the off-season expenses it was necessary for me to seek additional employment. As a journeyman carpenter, my skills and background opened a new opportunity for me to teach carpentry to inmates at the Bowden Institution. This would be a new experience for me, with a lot more procedures, rules and regulations, but I was up for the challenge. Having worked several years ago at the Drumheller Institution, I was acquainted with the prison environment in which I would be working Monday to Friday, on a contract until the end of March. It was a good fit.

I would be teaching first-year carpentry to a group of twelve men. This would involve both class time and instruction on how to use carpentry tools properly through hands-on building projects. Some people might be a little worried that inmates handing chisels, hammers, saws, nail guns, and other carpentry tools could put me in danger. As security is very high, and the training they gave me would help me out if the situation arose, I felt quite comfortable. The focus was not on why a man was in jail, but on teaching him a trade to better his life once he was released.

February was a very quiet month. but those few guests made being here very worthwhile.

"What a joy to find this wonderful treasure right in our backyard. This truly is a place of peace and rejuvenation. Thank you, Marcel and Randy for your gracious and generous hospitality. We will spread the word." Deborah and George, Edmonton, AB"

HEALING WEEKENDS WITH LEONARD MCCALLUM BOTH IN FEBRUARY AND MARCH continued to help us renew our souls and our purpose.

"What a nice place to find peace and let my mind relax, calm down and find what is in my heart. Randy and Marcel are such caring and kind men who take such good care of us. Our connection was amazing. Thank you for everything--the food, the care and for making me feel at home." Daniel

Friends introduced us to some to some new groups. The Red Deer Friendship Center staff had a retreat here. Another group with several ladies from Rocky Mountain House came to learn new techniques of relaxing and finding inner peace. Of course, they enjoyed the food!

"Thank you for being you!! You provided such a wonderful energy while we were here. Blessings." Lynda

This was also the time to go looking for business, so we went to Calgary to participate in the Body, Soul & Spirit Expo. This was an excellent opportunity to tell hundreds of people about the wonderful energy at the Lazy M Lodge and encourage them to come visit us. Next, we were off to capture a new market at the Body, Soul & Spirit Expo in Edmonton. These were very encouraging marketing experience. We had now put our name out across the province and in two of the largest city centres. We were feeling very confident that the Lazy M Lodge would become home to new people, but it would take time to see the results of these two promotional events.

Our booth at the Body, Soul & Spirit Expo

The countryside comes to life in May and June with gardening and lots of outdoor projects. One thing about the Lazy M Lodge is that there is no shortage of projects.

Yoga in the labyrinth is perfect for a spring day.

When fishing picks up The Fishin' Hole fly fishing school always brings a new group of people to experience all we have to offer. The July fly fishing school was a huge success and the weather was fantastic. Summer here is truly amazing, and to share it with others is what we are for. The North Raven River may be a challenging place to fish, but experiencing nature and learning something new is what many people enjoy here.

"Another visit to Paradise. I think this will be an annual break for us. The weather and the fishing cooperated. Stellar food and accommodations, as per usual. Thank-you, Randy and Marcel, for your amazing hospitality. See you next year!" Tony and Jamie, St. Albert AB

"As usual, the hospitality, meals, accommodation and fishing were amazing." Brian, Manager, Fishin' Hole, Edmonton AB

Having the Lodge, the hall, and lots of room on the grounds for camping, hosting family reunions is another part of the Lazy M Lodge that has become a great tradition. It makes a perfect setting for people to reconnect.

"We could not have found a better place to host our family gathering than the Lodge grounds and hall, and of course your hospitality is top notch." Ray, Faye, and Family

It was a warm sunny afternoon as many friends and family gathered together to witness Richard and Ashley get married. A wonderful ceremony on the front lawn and reception and dance in the hall made great memories for all who attended.

"We could not have had a more wonderful day, and Randy and Marcel you made it so easy for us and so memorable. Thanks so much." Richard and Ashley

Richard and Ashley's Wedding Day

Summertime is also about friends coming to visit, to camp, and to enjoy what we have. From swimming in the creek to barbecues on the deck, there's something fun to do for everyone.

"The Lazy M is now our new place to escape to and enjoy being out of the city. Such great accommodations, wonderful food, lots of room for camping and playing outdoor games. It just could not get any better. There is no other place like it." Fred, Edmonton

NATASHA AND CHAD CHOSE AUGUST 25TH TO EXCHANGE THEIR WEDDING VOWS. Many of their friends and family came to celebrate the outdoor wedding and enjoy festivities in the country hall.

"We could not have chosen a more awesome place for our big day. Thanks, you made it so easy." Chad and Natasha"

We felt so lucky when a honeymooning couple from France arrived to stay with us for a few days. Travelling to Canada was a new experience for them, and it was a new experience for us to showcase this part of the world.

"Our first impression of Canada was made so much more special because Randy and Marcel made us feel like family. It is hard for us to leave but we look forward to returning. Oh, and the fishing was amazing! How lucky you are to have this much nature right on your doorstep." Sebastian and Julie, Nancy, France

As the summer wrapped up, we saw the return of some old friends and met some new ones.

"Thanks for making a great weekend an amazing weekend, we love this place and we love you guys' energy. Until next time . . ." Jeff and Belen

"Thank you for a wonderful experience. The fishing was amazing, the accommodations were five star. I can't wait to come back." Jim Paris, France

"Once again, you have outdone yourselves. The bar can't get much higher. See you again next year." The Vegreville Ladies"

The Vegreville Ladies

"We know you are doing what is meant to be, offering a safe place for us to meet and reconnect. The grandfathers will bless us, and you, on this journey." The Louis Bull Tribe

Getting ready for one of the Native group healing weekends

When people gather around the dining room table we all feel like family. We may come from Edmonton, Saskatoon, Calgary, or Cape Cod, but sharing laughter and conversation is what creates memories.

"Another relaxing time. We feel so welcome here and the mix of guests is truly a wonderful and amazing experience." Sue, Shirley, Colleen, Lori and Marjorie

"Thanks for both a relaxing stay and for helping us arrange our fishing excursions. We had such stimulating conversations over great meals with great people. We look forward to coming back." Rich, Cape Cod, Main

October can be a bit of a gamble for good weather, but for Tricia and Tracy's October 13th wedding, this was not going to be a problem. It was a very sunny and warm fall day. Although most of the leaves were gone, there was beauty to be found everywhere.

Tracy and Tricia's wedding day

We were happy to host a particular event for a group from the Red Deer College. They find this to be a great space to hold their workshops and connect with their fellow staff.

"A wonderful place for our workshop. It regenerated us, rejuvenated us, and was the catalyst that we needed to move forward with our project. Such great food and a peaceful setting worked wonderfully for us." Scott

As we moved into late November, it was time to get ready for Christmas. And what better way can you get into the Christmas spirit than by hosting a Christmas decorating party?

"What a great idea, we had so much fun. Be sure to call us next year, as this was a great kick-off to the Christmas season." Tim, Karen, and family

Rusty and The Miller family

Our Christmas parties offer groups a barbecued steak dinner. Cooking twenty-four steaks on the barbecue at minus-thirty-degree weather depends on having a really warm jacket! Still, the Caroline Ambulance Society and the Rocky Dental office enjoyed the experience of a country Christmas with great food and friends.

When your family grows too big to have a Christmas house party, you can move them into the hall at the Lazy M Lodge. The Evans family has grown to over sixty members. The spacious hall, with its wood burning fireplace is ideal for this type of Christmas celebration.

"Thanks, Marcel and Randy. You have a great place for us to hold our annual Christmas party. We will be back next year. Hold our date!" Yvonne and families Caroline, AB

Ready for Christmas dinner

Christmas at the Lodge

As Christmas day approached, some of our family members joined us at the Lazy M Lodge to enjoy good food, company, and downtime.

On New Year's Eve we reflect back on the past year, see how our business has grown, and share that success with our close friends.

A moose checking out the place

LAZY M
DINNER RECIPES

Dinner time at the lazy M Lodge is truly a great time for fellowship.
When you get twenty people sitting around the large kitchen table
sharing food and stories, you know it's going to be a good time.

I have to start with our most requested recipe. It works great with
our steak or roast beef dinners. You can use lemon pepper seasoning
instead of the onion soup mix. Hopefully, you will have leftovers
that you can cut up and fry for delicious hash browns.

LAZY M HALF-BAKED ONION POTATOES

8-10 Yukon gold potatoes
2 tbsp onion soup mix
1 tbsp seasoning salt
4 tbsp olive oil

Preheat oven to 350°

Cut potatoes in half and place on well-olive-oiled cookie sheet. Combine onion soup mix and seasoning salt in a bowl. Dip oiled side of potato in dry mix to cover. Drizzle tops of potatoes with oil and sprinkle with dry mix. Bake for 40-45 minutes.

1/2 Baked Onion Potatoes

TURNIP AND APPLE CASSEROLE

1 medium turnip
1 tsp salt
1 tbsp butter
1½ cups apples, sliced
¼ cup brown sugar
1/8 tsp cinnamon

FOR THE TOPPING:
2 tbsp butter
2 tbsp brown sugar
1/3 cup flour
½ tsp salt

Preheat oven to 400°

Wash and peel turnip, cut into chunks. Add to boiling salt water and cook till tender. Drain and mash, adding 1 tablespoon of butter. Mix apples, brown sugar, and cinnamon with the turnips and place in a greased 9 x 13 casserole dish. Mix brown sugar, sugar and salt and sprinkle on top. Bake for 30 minutes. Yield: 6-8 servings.

LAZY M CHICKEN PARMESAN

4-6 skinless boneless chicken breasts
2 eggs
4 cups Panko crumbs
2 tbsp Montreal Chicken Seasoning
½ cup grated Parmesan
2 tablespoons flour
1 cup olive oil for frying
½ cup tomato sauce
¼ cup grated fresh mozzarella or swiss cheese (or smoked cheddar)
¼ cup fresh basil
½ cup provolone
¼ cup Parmesan cheese

Preheat oven to 450°

Place chicken breast between two sheets of plastic or parchment paper and pound until half an inch thick. Season with salt, pepper, and Montreal Chicken Seasoning. Beat eggs and set aside. Mix bread crumbs and Parmesan cheese in a separate bowl and set aside. Place flour in a bowl and coat both sides of the chicken breast before dipping in eggs and then Panko and parmesan, pressing onto both sides. In a skillet, heat 1 cup of olive oil over medium heat until it begins to shimmer. Cook chicken until golden brown--about two minutes on each side. Place the chicken in a large baking dish or pan, spoon one third of the tomato sauce over chicken breasts with equal amounts of cheese, fresh basil, provolone. Sprinkle with Parmesan on top and drizzle with olive oi. Bake 20-25 minutes, until the cheese is bubbly and the chicken breasts reach the internal temperature of 165°.

BARBECUED SALMON WITH
SUN-DRIED TOMATOES

1 medium-sized salmon, filleted
4 tbsp Clubhouse Salmon Seasoning
8 tbsp sun-dried tomatoes

Preheat oven to 350°

Onto tin foil sprinkle 2 tablespoons of with 4 tablespoons of chopped sun-dried tomatoes. Lay the salmon fillet on the mixture. Repeat seasoning and sun-dried tomatoes on top. Seal tinfoil edges tightly. Cook on a barbecue and turn after seven minutes, for a total of 14 minutes, or until tinfoil expands. Internal salmon temperature should be 160° with caramelization of the sun-dried tomatoes and the seasoning. Serve with rice, carrots, and spinach salad.

LAZY M GRILLED VEGETABLES

4 cups broccoli florets
4 cups cauliflower florets
2 cups carrots cut into strips
½ cup green peppers, chopped
½ cup red peppers, chopped
½ cup celery, chopped
¼ cup onion, chopped
4 tbsp olive oil
2 tbsp Italian seasoning
4 tbsp butter
2 tbsp lemon juice

Cut and wash all vegetables. Stir in all the seasonings and wrap tightly in tinfoil. Place on the barbecue at 350° and turn every 5-10 minutes. Once the tinfoil has puffed up, remove from barbecue and serve.

LAZY M CORN AND BASIL

4 cans corn
1 red pepper, chopped
½ cup celery, chopped
½ cup onion, chopped
4 tbsp butter
1 tbsp garlic
1 tbsp of dried basil leaves
salt and pepper to taste

Cook onion and celery in a medium saucepan until tender. Mix in the corn, celery, and onion. Add butter and seasonings. Stir frequently until it is heated through, and serve.

BAKED NUTMEG CARROTS

4 cups carrots, sliced
½ cup water
6 tbsp of butter
2 tbsp of sugar
1 tsp of nutmeg
1 tsp of salt

Preheat oven to 350°

Spread the carrots evenly in a 9 x 12 casserole dish and add water. Sprinkle with the nutmeg, sugar and salt and dab on the butter. Bake 15-20 minutes, or until carrots are soft.

CHAPTER 4
2013

NEW YEAR'S DAY BEGAN WITH SEVERAL FRIENDS RECOVERING FROM THE party the night before.

Bookings in January and February were quiet, giving us the chance to do small renovations and other projects. We made new headboards and side tables and did a major spring cleaning. I was also working Monday to Friday, teaching at the Bowden institution.

Our weekend guests were from staff and board retreats for Safe Harbour, a group from the Red Deer Native Friendship Center, as well as a men's group from Edmonton.

A phone call in late February brought the news that we had been nominated for the Rocky Chamber of Commerce and the Clearwater County Hospitality Award for 2012. On March 1st a dinner would be held in Rocky Mountain House. That evening after dinner, it was announced that we had won. We had been in very good company for the running, and we felt honoured. It also gave our services good exposure to our local area.

Clearwater County Hospitality Award

Randy and Marcel accepting their award

March was also the month that we broke into the "quilting retreat" market. Suzanne had organized fourteen ladies to come for three days of quilting and exchanging ideas and stories while checking out the Lazy M.

"What a great place! So glad we found it. The food was great, the hosts were fabulous, and the facility for our quilting was top notch. We will see you again next year!" Susanne and gals

Quilters

By April and May we were ready for all the snow to melt away. Some guests stayed with us while attending Lane's Hoof Care course. Others were just here for a getaway.

"Thank you for a great weekend. The peace and quiet was just what I needed, and the food was amazing. Looking forward to coming back soon." Deanna, Bragg Creek AB

The Fishin' Hole was back with sixteen students for their annual June fly fishing school.

"What a genuine wild Alberta experience, complete with the rural charm, lots of wildlife, and the perfect creek to learn how to fly fish. Next time I plan to get that fish!" Chris, Edmonton

The Fishin' Hole Class of 2013

We try to make sure that when guests from other countries come for a stay, their experience here at the Lazy M represents the best in Alberta.

"Absolutely the best accommodations I've had between Berlin and Vancouver. We will be back." Ernst, Berlin Germany

We were now getting to the point in our business that we felt confident booking groups for corporate and business meetings. One thing the Lazy M has to offer is a quiet meeting place, central to most of the province. In June we had guests from as far north as Peace River and as far south as Medicine Hat, and all points between.

"Loved the energy, the calm, the wonderful hospitality, and the amazing hosts. Thank you for putting up with all of us. We look forward already to our next retreat in 2014." Heather, Edmonton

Local groups, like the Rocky Mountain House quilting ladies, enjoy the ease of getting here. They love the privacy, and they are extremely happy with the hall and how well it works for them. The Lodge is very comfortable and even though most of them could drive home, they prefer to stay as a group and spend time playing games, quilting, and getting to know each other.

"I can't say enough how perfect this place is for our quilting group. The lodge and the food are five star, and what you've done to that barn that makes it into such a beautiful space for us to quilt is amazing. We look forward to coming back in the fall and again next summer." Cindy, Rocky Mountain House

When you get eight couples together for golf and fun, it can't get much better than at the Lazy M.

"We so enjoyed the comforts of home and the awesome meals. Could not believe how many great golf courses are in the area, and so close. This is our new go-to place. Thanks, Randy and Marcel. We will be back." Bruce and the gang, Westlock AB

Much introspection that has been done here at the Lazy M. . . .

"We have deep gratitude for your impeccable integrity during our stay. We felt safe, provided for, and nourished by your wonderful food. Your presence, big hearts, and your wonderful smiles made this weekend so special. Thank-you so much." Vireo, Calgary

One could not ask for a better place to host a week-long painting group. Dave More and twelve other artists arrived Sunday, July 7th. This talented group of people were here to capture the images that presented themselves all around the Lazy M Lodge. The beauty we experience every day, and the great weather and awesome company inspired these people. At five-thirty every evening the group gathered at the hall with a glass of wine to review everyone's artwork of the day. There were so many styles of painting, and awesome interpretations of the landscape.

"Wow! our first time here. This is really one of the best-kept secrets in the West. It was beyond our wildest dreams. Randy and Marcel, you are first class. Thank-you for the awesome meals and the wonderful hospitality. You really did treat us like family. Can't wait until next year." Patty and Tony, Red Deer

Dave reviewing the day's paintings

During the summer months, as one group leaves, another group arrives. The July Fishin' Hole fly fishing school was again another complete sellout. The weather was exceptional and the fishing was fantastic.

"I love the Lazy M, and from what I can see you guys are anything but lazy. Thanks for the wonderful food and hospitality. I will certainly be back." Louise, Calgary

It's really nice to have our family and friends come to visit us. My mom, Jean, was very happy to have her sister and some other friends from Drumheller come out and see what we have done.

"Randy and Marcel, i marvel at what you have created. You truly have built something special and now i see why you are kept so busy. The accommodations are top notch, the food amazing. I wish you nothing but more success, and can't wait to return." Dorothy B., Drumheller AB

"A delightful experience with outstanding food and absolutely beautiful surroundings." Bert and Anne, Drumheller

Hosting White Thunderbird Healing and our friends from the First Nations community is a great time for everyone to seek some guidance from the grandfathers.

"This is an amazing place with amazing energy and amazing people. Thank-you so much." Donna

"Grateful to have found a new paradise and to reconnect with nature." Cora

"This is a great place for our family reunion. We have family from all over, and to be able to gather here to visit, sit around the campfire, sing songs and enjoy the beautiful long weekend, we could not have asked for anything better." The Spierenburg Family

The Smith family came together from Vancouver to Atlanta Georgia and all points in between to spend a few days enjoying good food and drink, and catching up during the long summer days.

"We could not have found a better spot for us to reconnect and make memories as a family. Thanks." Doug

The garden in the round pen

Amy and Jason had picked August 17th for their wedding day. Blue skies and warm temperatures welcomed the guests from as far away as Mill Bay British Columbia, Saskatoon Saskatchewan, and Saint John, New Burnswick

"The perfect place for our wedding! Thank-you so much for all you have done to make this such a special weekend. Amy and Jason"

On August 24th, the special day that Corey and Angela exchanged their vows, many friends and family came to witness their commitment.

"We cannot thank you enough, Randy and Marcel, for helping us make this one of the best days of our lives. Our family and friends so enjoyed the beautiful facility that you have created." Corey and Angela

We had the pleasure of hosting a very avid fisherman from Paris, France. He spent a week with us, hiring a fishing guide who took him to several spots in the area. On Friday, August 30, he decided to go out on his own to conquer the North Raven River. We loaded up Francois and his fishing gear at eight a.m., and took him about 10 km down stream from the Lodge. In most cases eight hours should be plenty of time to fish back up to the Lazy M Lodge. When seven o'clock arrived and he had not yet returned, we began to get a little concerned. By eight o'clock it was time to start looking for him. I set out walking downstream and Marcel called Rocky Search and Rescue. At nine o'clock the sun was starting to set and there was still no sign of our Parisian fisherman. I had walked three miles downstream and had been calling out his name for over an hour. Then, at ten o'clock I got a reply. Out of the bush and across a stream came a very weary fisherman. I called Marcel to let him know that I had found Francois and to call off the search. By the time we got back to the Lodge, it was almost ten-thirty, and our fisherman was very tired and hungry!

"Many thanks to Marcel and Randy for the top-notch food and accommodation. Your care and concern for my safety and my well-being is so much appreciated. Next time I visit I will be sure to always have a guide with me. See you in a couple of years. Francois." Paris, France

September brings those guests returning to find peace, comfort and tranquillity.

"Once again, a fantastic experience for us at the Lazy M. Thank you for your love, your kindness, your support and your willingness to share, as well as the wonderful food and the top-notch accommodations." Scott, Red Deer College

AND THE RETURN OF OLD FRIENDS IS SOMETHING WE LOOK SO FORWARD TO!

"It's like coming home. You guys treated us so well. See you next year." Lorie, Marjorie, Sue. Shirley, Colleen

"It just gets better every year!" The Vegreville Ladies

The Vegreville Ladies playing in the leaves

Fall weddings are so special here. Terry and Ryan found the perfect day to hold their wedding. Friends and family gathered on a day when the temperature was a perfect eighteen degrees to witness this couple begin their new lives.

"Everyone so enjoyed all that the Lazy M has to offer. Truly the best place to have a wedding." Terry and Ryan

It was time for a "glorious girls weekend getaway." Jeanette had a very memorable weekend in store for sixteen awesome ladies, experiencing nature and sharing the comforts of home.

"The energy of this place was perfect for my retreat. I will be sure to re-book again soon." Janette

"You have created a special place. It's comfortable and refreshing. The food was awesome, not to mention the great friendships made this past weekend. Thanks so much!" Deborah, Calgary

"Don't forget, what happens at the Lazy M, stays at the lazy M." Carol

Mother cat and her family

When you get a phone call for a booking and the lady on the phone is telling you that they are a bunch of retired hookers, you really don't know how to respond. The caller then explained they are crafty ladies who enjoy rug hooking. I knew we could handle this group.

"We will be back again! The food, the rooms, and the hall were all first rate. We sure love this place. Cheryl"

Rusty looking after one of mother cat's kittens

It started to snow on November 3rd and just would not stop. But, this was winter in Alberta and you still have to go ahead and plan your Christmas party. Several groups such as the Rocky Financial Friends, the Rocky Funeral Home, and the Caroline Ambulance Society were booking parties with us. Also, we would be hosting the celebration of our neighbour Audrey's 75th birthday party.

This was a busy time for us, and I had not been feeling well. Marcel tried to get me to the hospital in Rocky on Sunday, December 8th but we were unable to get through the blizzard that was upon us. So, early on Monday, December 9th, Marcel broke trail to get to Rocky Mountain House Health Center. After a few tests, it was determined that my gallbladder was very inflamed and swollen and that I needed to go by ambulance to Red Deer Regional Hospital for surgery as soon as possible. By ten a.m. on December 10th, I was in recovery. The doctor said I was very lucky, but he was pleased with the way the surgery had gone.

The next question was, would I be able to attend a holiday with my family in Tulum, Mexico? We were to leave Saturday morning. Having my daughter as a nurse as would be the only way I would be permitted to go. So, I packed my bags and with my mother and with my two kids' assistance, we flew out of Calgary for 10 days on the beach at the resort. It may sound all well and fine, but I was only able to eat and drink small amounts, and I just lay around healing in thirty-degree temperatures.

Marcel had been left behind to hold down the fort until I returned on December 25th. During those 10 days, while I rested and got better, Marcel "enjoyed" keeping the yard and the laneway clear during several days of heavy snow. We enjoyed Christmas Day evening and Boxing Day with family, and we were able to get ready for our next group, arriving on December 27th.

Trudy and Jim and twenty members of their blended family took time to celebrate Christmas and enjoy everything that the Lazy M Lodge has to offer.

"Absolutely the best hospitality and food ever. No one wants to leave. Thank-you, and we look forward to seeing you again in two years." Trudy and Jim and family

On December 31st, several of our close friends joined us for a potluck supper, games and fireworks, and yes, outdoor hot tubbing, in minus twenty-five-degree temperatures. What a wonderful evening, and a great way to start 2014.

Twin moose calves, checking out the place

BEGIN EACH DAY WITH A GREATFUL HEART

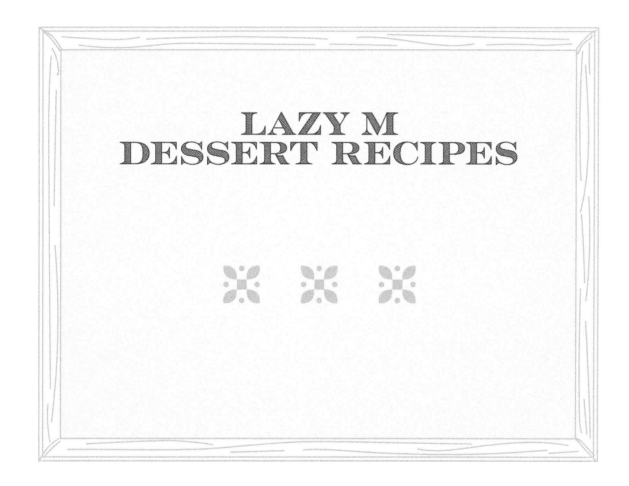

LAZY M
DESSERT RECIPES

PEACH COBBLER

4 cups frozen or fresh peaches
¾ cup sugar
1 cup flour
1¼ tsp baking powder
4 tbsp butter
½ cup milk
1 tbsp cornstarch
1 cup sugar
1 tsp vanilla
½ tsp salt
1 cup boiling water

Preheat oven to 350°

Pour peaches in a greased 9 x 13 pan. Combine ¾ cup sugar, 1 cup flour, and baking powder. Add melted butter, milk and stir until a dough forms. Spread over top of peaches. Mix cornstarch, sugar, salt, and vanilla with boiling water. Pour this over the topping. Bake for one hour or until golden brown. Serve with ice cream.

LAZY MAN'S RASPBERRY PIE

1 frozen pie crust
4-5 cups fresh or frozen raspberries
1 cup sugar
3 tbsp cornstarch
1½ cups cold water
3 tbsp corn syrup
¼ cup raspberry or strawberry jello powder mix.
½ tsp vanilla extract

Pre-bake pie shell as per instructions. In a saucepan combine sugar, cornstarch, water, and stir until smooth. Add corn syrup. Bring to a boil, and cook for two minutes or until smooth. Remove from heat and add vanilla, gelatin and stir until dissolved. Cool at room temperature for about 30 minutes. Stir in raspberries with sauce, then pour into pie crust. Chill for 3 hours. Serve with whipped cream.

OATMEAL COCONUT COOKIES

1 cup butter
1 cup sugar
1 cup brown sugar
2 eggs
2 tsp vanilla
1 tsp salt
1 tsp baking powder
1 tsp baking soda
2½ cups flour
2 cups oatmeal
1 cup of coconut

Preheat oven to 350°

Beat butter, sugars, eggs and vanilla until creamy. Mix dry ingredients separately and combine with butter and eggs for a cookie dough. Drop on cookie sheet from spoon or ice cream scoop. Bake for 8-10 minutes.

EASY LAZY M CHEESE CAKE

CRUST

1 ½ cups chocolate wafer crumbs

2 tbsp sugar

1/3 cup melted butter

FILLING

8 oz of semi-sweet chocolate, melted

½ cup milk

1 package of softened cream cheese

2 tablespoons sugar

4 cups Cool Whip (one tub)

Press crust into a 9" springform pan. Mix cream cheese, sugar, ¼ cup milk and 5 squares of melted chocolate until smooth. Stir in the cool whip until blended. Pour into pan. Mix the remaining 3 melted chocolate squares melt with the ¼ cup milk and pour over the top of the cake in a thin layer..

To add a unique taste, add two tablespoons of instant coffee powder to the cool whip.

Another option is to make a regular graham cracker crust. Then, take 1 can of pumpkin pie filling, ½ cup sugar, ½ tsp of pumpkin pie spice, and mix all together with the tub of Cool Whip. Pour on the pie crust and cool for three hours. When serving, drizzle with caramel or chocolate.

EASY APPLE CRISP

12 cups of cut apple slices
1¼ cups white sugar
2 heaping tablespoons flour
1¼ teaspoons cinnamon
½ cup water
1½ cup quick oats
1½ cup flour
1¼ cup brown sugar
¼ tsp baking powder
¼ tsp baking soda
½ cup melted butter

Preheat oven to 350°

Mix apples, sugar, flour and water and place in a 9 x13 baking pan. Combine oats, flour and the rest of the ingredients together until you have a crumbly mix. Pack it down on top of the apples. Bake for about 45 minutes or until the pan is bubbling with goodness

ADULT RICE CRISPY TREATS

4 cups large marshmallows
4 tbsp butter
5 cups Rice Crispies
1 oz of Irish cream

Place marshmallows and butter in a sprayed or lightly-buttered plastic bowl and microwave for 1 minute or until soft and fluffy. Thoroughly mix in the Rice Crispies and then add Irish Cream. Pack down in lightly-buttered 9 x13 pan and refrigerate. Be sure to serve cold with a good cup of coffee.

LAZY MAN'S BLACK FOREST CAKE

1 chocolate cake mix
1 can cherry pie filling
1 tub Cool Whip
1 package chocolate pudding mix
½ cup shaved chocolate

Bake cake as per instructions in a 9 x13 cake pan. Cool and cut cake into individual portions on plates. Make the pudding and chill. Half cake pieces horizontally. On the bottom, place one scoop of pudding and one of cool whip. Cover with cake top, cherry pie filling, chocolate shavings. Simple, but so good.

LAZY MAN'S CARROT CAKE

4 eggs
1½ cups vegetable oil
2 tsp vanilla extract
2 cups white sugar
2 cups flour
2 tsp baking soda
2 tsp baking powder
½ tsp salt
2 tsp cinnamon
3 cups grated carrots
1 cup crushed pineapple, drained

Preheat oven to 350°

Prepare a 9 x 13 cake pan. Combine eggs, oil, sugar, vanilla. Separately, mix dry ingredients together well. Add dry mixture to wet, alternating carrots and pineapple to form batter. Bake for 40-50 minutes. Cool on wire rack.

For traditional frosting, beat together 2 x 8 ounce packs cream cheese with ½ cup softened butter.

Beat in two cups of confectioners' sugar and a teaspoon of vanilla extract until fluffy.

DETOURS, CHALLENGES, AND CRISIS, ARE
SIMPLY COVERS FOR MIRACLES THAT
HAD NO OTHER WAY OF REACHING YOU.

CHAPTER 5
2014

THE OUTLOOK FOR 2014 WAS GREAT. LOCAL BUSINESSES WERE SHOWING interest in the after-Christmas party concept. The "chicks" from Pure Hair design in Caroline enjoy spending time here together as friends outside of their work environment.

The quilting groups were regrouping and our Beaver Creek Mercantile friends happily gathered to spend four days on quilting projects, balancing fun and productivity. They enjoyed sewing in the hall with a roaring fire in the fireplace. We enjoy hosting these creative ladies and keeping them comfortable and well fed.

Regular business retreats with the Safe Harbour group from Red Deer are always fun.

February tends to be about spring cleaning. Washing walls, floors, bedding, painting, touch-ups, repairs and regular maintenance helps keep the Lodge fresh and ready for guests. Sometimes, our visitors are attending a local program, such as Lane's Barefoot Hoof Care course, where they learn how to properly trim hooves.

Finally, the long winter ended in March, Record amounts of snow had fallen and the large melt threatened to cause flooding around the house. We dug trenches to direct the runoff to the creek.

Rusty, enjoying the view from the bridge on the North Raven River

The hall was put to great use as a work space by crafting groups interested on holding events for scrap booking, sewing, painting, furniture refinishing, and the like.

"Everything was so great from the time we arrived until the time we left. The food was wonderful, the work space truly awesome, and you guys take such good care of us. See you in the fall!" Bobbie and crew.

Spring crafting and quilting

In March, guests find the Lazy M Lodge is the place for personal time to relax and make plans.

"Thanks for helping us plan our wedding this summer. We are feeling really great about the choice we made." Dan and Megan, Red Deer

The quilters, it seems, never stop! We are their home away from home.

"We are so glad to be back. Your hall is so perfect for the fourteen of us to quilt and enjoy a weekend away. You guys really know how to treat us." Linda M, Calgary

Quilters hard at work

"So glad to be back for our second retreat. It has been an amazing weekend and you guys look after us so well. Thanks." Diane, Rocky Mountain House.

We were looking forward to our annual participation in the Body, Soul & Spirit Expo in Edmonton, which has helped us make new business connections.

Relaxing by the outdoor fireplace, guests began to come in April to enjoy the signs of spring as the snow disappeared. The outdoor fireplace draws people together for conversation and wine.

Board planning retreats from all over the province remain popular, such as with our regular clients, the Safe Harbour Society and the Alberta Library Trustees Association.

"Once again, our meetings and time here for fellowship only get better with great food and this wonderful Lodge. You guys do an amazing job. Thanks." Heather

Students from the Three Hills School graduating class of 2014 were amazing. Accompanied by chaperones they created wonderful memories and we were proud to be a part of this time in their lives.

2014 Grads enjoying the Lazy M

June: outdoor groups and fly fishing, and family and friends celebrating being together!

We were happy to host Scott and Jackie's 25th wedding anniversary. Guests camped or stayed in the Lodge. The weekend was filled with music, laughter, and new memories.

"Thanks guys for making this occasion even more special. All our friends and family enjoyed your wonderful place." Scott and Jackie

June 21st was when Mary and Aaron exchanged vows along the beautiful banks of the North Raven River.

Mary and Aaron's wedding day

"The perfect place for a wedding. Marcel and Randy, you were so helpful with every little detail, and made it so easy. Thanks for everything." Mary and Aaron

Friday afternoon in June brings the fly fishing schools. As the students arrive, they begin to relax and meet their fellow students and instructors for a briefing. They will learn how to tie knots, use equipment and learn some of the techniques of the fly fishing sport.

Class time for the new fly fisherman

"Could not have asked for a better weekend. I learned so much, and the food and the location is perfect. Looking forward to returning again soon." Joe, Fort McMurray AB

Family reunions are great, especially when they are yours! My mom's family, the Coads, gathered to reconnect after many years.

"Randy and Marcel have created an ideal place for family reunions. We sure look forward to doing this again soon." Ed and Linda Green Valley, Arizona

The Coad Family reunion

The Lamoreaux, family came to enjoy camping and lots of fun outdoor activities. The Leboldus, family also converged here and enjoyed making memories around the campfire.

"Just when you think that, yes, you've seen it all, no, you haven't. The Lazy M was like coming home. It was everything and more that we needed for our family reunion. Keep up the good work. We will see you soon!" Michael and family

A group of twelve talented artists returned for a week of amazing painting, inspired by the beautiful July weather. A beautiful piece of artwork was gifted to the Lazy M for guests to admire.

A gift from the Artist Retreat group.

"Thanks for a wonderful week, you guys run a great place." Dave M., Benalto

We sometimes host lunches here, such as for the ladies from the Rocky Mountain House "Red Hat" group, who enjoyed an afternoon of lunch followed by tea beside the creek.

"Truly, one of our best outings yet!" Jean, Rocky Mountain House

The quilters know how to live! They come and go as they like from the Lazy M throughout the year while creating some amazing works of art.

"Can't thank you both enough. We can't wait to come back next year and see what you have done. Get going on writing a cookbook!" Diana M., Iqaluit Nunavut

Diana's "Old Friends" quilting group

We certainly enjoy a variety of visitors. When we get guests from other countries we realize what a special place we have here in Alberta.

"We just had a one night stop here, but we have to say it was the best part of our holiday. This place invites you to slow down and relax. Very friendly hosts, great food and interesting chats have made such a lovely memory on this vacation. Thanks for everything." Daniela, Switzerland

Summer storms in Alberta are amazing to watch, but none so amazing as on August 6th. It was hot and muggy, and in the distance were approaching black clouds. As the afternoon moved on we kept our eye to the sky. The wind picked up from the north and we could see this was going to be more than just a rain shower. The thunder was deafening, and the falling raindrops were lit up by lightning. It was time to make sure all our guests and their vehicles were safe.

Everyone gathered underneath in the shelter of the veranda so we could watch the storm. The wind rose. The heavy rain changed to pea-sized hail and grew to marble-sized. Then, the hail came down as golf balls and the damage began. Next, the sound of ice tennis balls on the tin roof was incredibly loud. The enormous hail stripped the leaves from the trees and the flower gardens were smashed to the ground. Heavy rains and wind followed, but within thirty minutes the storm had moved off.

There was damage to the roof, broken windows, broken skylights, the yard looked like a war zone, and water was running everywhere. The power of Mother Nature's fury is amazing. The thing is, she doesn't stick around to help clean up.

Now, this happened on a Wednesday as Marcel's daughter Michelle and her future husband Matt were to be married on Saturday afternoon on the front lawn. Help poured in from friends, neighbours, and relatives who raked leaves and restored the bedding plants and flowers. By Friday, I had fixed the roofs and replaced the broken glass and sky lights. As wedding guests arrived on Friday, there was very little evidence of the Wednesday hailstorm.

There can be no more special day then when a dad gives away his daughter to a loving man. We were so happy that Matt and Michelle, and all of their family and friends, chose to share their special day here at the Lazy M.

We served dinner in the hall to 125 people. A dance, followed by a beautiful Alberta evening, put the finishing touches on the perfect day and the perfect weekend

"Where to start? We held our wedding here at the Lazy M Lodge and it was absolutely perfect. The guests were awestruck with the entire place. The hospitality they were shown, the great food, and the venue couldn't have been any better. Our version of the perfect wedding!

Everything looked great. A weekend to remember for 100+ people. Thank-you so much!" Mr. and Mrs. Matt Wilson, Calgary, AB

Matt and Michelle's Wedding

Our friends and regular guests, from Sherwood Park, came back to spend a few days resting, relaxing, and recharging.

"So nice to have found a place that feels like our second home. Great hospitality wonderful food. Thanks, Marcel and Randy. We will see you again soon." George and Deborah

When Dan and Megan visited us in the summer of 2013 they were excited to have booked their wedding day for August 16th at one of their favourite places.

"Thank you so much for making our wedding day dreams come true. You two are amazing hosts. I know that our guests had a wonderful time! We will be back for many more visits." Dan and Megan, Red Deer.

Dan and Megan getting married on the front lawn

Sometimes a note in our guest book says it all.

"The saying 'there is no place like home' has been disproved at the- Lazy M Lodge. It can equal, even surpass the great food and comfort of home. Amazing setting. Thank you for this wonderful escape and experience." Alan P

When the Spruce View School approached us to host their staff orientation, we were excited that the hall was set up for meetings. To meet outside school was an interesting experience for teachers gearing up for the new school year. After a long day of school staff changed into formal wear for dinner and what they referred to as "Oscar night." Everyone enjoyed a lovely meal and unique ambiance.

A red carpet was rolled out to the front of the podium, and the principal of the school announced the first award of the current "Oscar winners."

" . . . and the Outstanding Hospitality Award goes to Randy and Marcel of the Lazy M Lodge!"

We were quite surprised we had won this, and approached the podium to receive it.

The principal introduced us with a little speech: "These two gentlemen took a huge risk in life to follow their dream. They worked hard, believed in their new venture, and trusted in each other. Today, they are very successful and happy with where they are in their life's journey. There is a lesson here for you, fellow teachers. We need to encourage our students to believe in themselves and to follow their dreams. Thanks, guys, for being a great example of how to believe in yourselves and love life."

Truly, this was one of the most moving moments we had ever had as proprietors of the Lazy M. Again, it validated that we were guided to do what we were doing.

Spruce View School Award

On the last weekend in August, Brad and Krissy, had everything ready for their wedding, which took place on August 30th . It was another sunny, warm August day as family and friends gathered for their wedding.

" A dream has come true, as everything we planned for came together at the Lazy M Lodge. So happy to have had Marcel and Randy make us and our guests feel so welcome." Brad and Krissy

As the days got shorter and evenings cooler, it was still a wonderful time of year to get married. Cody and Sarah held their wedding here at the Lazy M Lodge. Sarah was raised in Australia and met Cody while working in Canada. Having wedding guests come from Australia was very special for us.

"We so enjoyed the Lazy M. The hospitality and the setting for this wedding was beyond perfect. We will recommend it to all our friends in Sydney, Australia." George and Colleen"

Cody and Sarah's Wedding Day

The fall is a time when businesses and organizations get back to doing business. A retreat here at the Lazy M Lodge for the Brazeau County Council, helped get staff and council members get back into the groove.

"It is the perfect place to meet, and nice hosts and great food. It was very productive, yet relaxing." Anthony, Drayton Valley.

On September 9th weekend the amazing Vegreville Ladies returned for their fifth year of friendship with us. They've been coming to the Lazy M for eighteen years!

The Vegreville Ladies

The gals of the Beaver Creek quilters group were also happy to be back, making the hall buzz with sewing machines and lots of chatter. Sometimes the four days does not seem enough time, but as many a quilter will tell, they're never done, anyway.

The women of the Beaver Creek quilting group

Unexpected guests are always a nice surprise, like the honeymoon couple from Vancouver who were making their way across the country.

"These were the best and most enjoyable few days of our honeymoon. Such great hosts, the food was amazing, the peace and quiet was perfect. Thanks! We look forward to coming back." Alex and Merioum

The twelve dedicated quilters of the 'Stitch in Time" group also started off October for us.

"What a wonderful, relaxing home. Such wonderful food and great company." Anne

October is also a time when guests come to get the last of the good weather. Our good friends Shirley and Sue from Saskatoon, Marjorie and Lori from Edmonton, and Colleen from Calgary met here for their annual few days of catching up. They have so much fun here and in the area, shopping and going to tourist stops. It has become one of their most favorite places.

"Starting with the wonderful welcome, it is like coming home. We have so many wonderful memories that we made here over the last five years. Looking forward to making many more." Marjorie, Edmonton.

The Labyrinth Ladies

Cindy and her Board of Directors from the Rocky Mountain House Chamber of Commerce sometimes take weekdays to strategize, enjoy good food and a collegial atmosphere. Another group from Edmonton also took a couple of days to have their meetings here.

"Thanks for the hospitality, friendliness, and engagement. This is a great facility with great food and is so unique and refreshing. We look forward to returning in the near future for more retreats." Dave, Edmonton

Hunters come out to make the Lazy M their home base for a few days at the beginning of November. They leave early for a day of scouting and tracking, returning for a hearty meal and to relax in the hot tub.

The talented group of happy Rug Hookers return, too.

The Rug Hookers group

Rug Hookers Projects

Crafters, quilters, and rug hookers try to complete projects on a "get it done weekend" before Christmas, here at Lazy M Lodge.

"I have to say we had a very productive weekend completing several projects, but also enjoyed great food, comfortable beds, and awesome company. One of our highlights was to have Ashley here to offer massages to some of us that had sore shoulders and backs from spending hours bending over our sewing machines! We will certainly do that on our next retreat. See you in the spring." Suzanne, Innisfail

It was December again, and time to decorate the Lodge for Christmas celebrations of local businesses like Royal Lepage and Everything H2O from Rocky Mountain House, the staff and family of the Alberta Conservation Association, and our friends from Longhurst Trucking. They enjoyed a beautiful Christmas setting, wonderful food, stayed over after a late party, and had breakfast the next morning. We thank you for your business.

We also found time to spend happy times with our families here at the Lazy M as Christmas approached. Both my and Marcel's families gather at the Lazy M Lodge during this season. Everyone pitches in and helps with the cooking and cleaning, and then we have fun playing some good old card games, relaxing around the wood burning stove, telling stories, and just enjoying the moments.

New Year's always brings our men's social group together for our annual potluck dinner, with drinks, games, good conversations, and, of course, fireworks at midnight. This is always a good way to end one year and welcome the next.

Christmas lights outside the Lodge

A New Year!

As we reflect on our first five years at the Lazy M Lodge, words cannot express how truly blessed we have been on this journey so far. From our first guests in 2010, we have seen a steady growth over the years and have made lifelong friends.

Every day brings someone new to stay. When we see it through their experience, we are reminded how special the Lazy M Lodge is. Making memories here is just part of the magic. Thank-you for being a part of this experience so far.

The neighbours at Christmas: Lane, Margie, Natascha, Kate, Randy, Marcel

OFTEN, HAVING WHAT YOU WANT
IS A FUNCTION OF LETTING
GO OF WHAT YOU HAVE.

LAZY M
SAUCES AND
COOKING TIPS

We have learned a lot, and would like to share some of the highlights.

STEAK MARINADE

½ cup water
½ cup olive oil
¼ cup soya sauce
¼ cup red wine vinegar
¼ cup lemon juice
1 tbsp meat tenderizer
1 tbsp minced garlic
2 tbsp Dijon mustard
3 tbsp Montreal steak spice
3 tbsp Worcestershire sauce

Put ingredients into a blender and process until mixed. Pour over steak, turning pieces as required over 6 hours. May be made ahead and stored. Discard used marinade. Preheat BBQ to 400°. Sear steaks 4 minutes each side. Internal temperature should be 130° for medium rare and 140° for medium.

MUSTARD SAUCE FOR BAKED HAM

2 tbsp ground mustard
1/3 cup white vinegar
1 cup sugar
2 eggs
¼ tsp salt

Combine ingredients in a saucepan. Slowly bring to boil until the sauce thicken.

Serve with baked ham.

HOMEMADE CRANBERRY SAUCE

2 cups dried cranberries
2 cups water
¼ cup sugar
1 tbsp lemon juice

Combine all ingredients in a saucepan over medium heat and stir until it boils and thickens. Use immersion blender to give smooth consistency. Serve with turkey.

HOMEMADE FRENCH DRESSING

Salad dressings may be processed in a blender or simply shaken in a container.

¼ cup olive oil
¼ cup maple syrup
¼ cup Dijon mustard
1/3 cup lemon juice
1/3 cup red wine vinegar
½ tbsp minced garlic

HONEY GINGER DRESSING

1 cup olive oil
½ cup lemon juice
½ cup honey
1 tbsp finely grated ginger
1 tbsp Dijon mustard
1 tbsp minced garlic
salt and pepper to taste

HOMEMADE TOMATO SAUCE

1 cup olive oil
8 cups roma tomatoes, cut in half
2 tbsp basil
2 tbsp oregano
salt and pepper

On an oiled cookie sheet, put halved tomatoes cut side down. Sprinkle seasoning on top and add drizzles of olive oil. Bake for an hour at 250°. When soft, blend to a smooth consistency. Pour in freezer bags and freeze flat. Great for any recipe requiring tomato sauce.

SIMPLE TIPS

For an all-purpose cleaning spray, we mix:
2 oz dawn dish soap
4 oz lemon juice
8 oz white vinegar
10 oz water.

Mix up and pour in spray bottle, or use to clean directly. Works on all cleaning surfaces including stove top and oven.

- For extra assurance that kitchen items are properly sanitized, we use 1 oz bleach to 10 oz water. Use this to clean counter tops and cutting boards.

- Spider and Pest Control
Mix 1 teaspoon of peppermint extract with 1 litre of water in a spray bottle. Spray where spider webs appear, or wipe on where spiders like to hang out. May be regularly re-applied. We have also found this to be very good to deter mice. Spray around buildings or any place Mice seem to be present, and the odour will discourage them from entering.

- "Buzz-Off" Fly Traps
Boil 1 cup of water, add ½ cup sugar and ½ cup vinegar. Fill small mason jam jars half full. Drill 3-4 ¼ " holes in the lids before attaching. Wrap a 2" strip of yellow construction paper around the jar. Place it on a window ledge or areas where flies seem to be a problem.

CHAPTER 6

Lane and Margie Moore had an idea back in 1990. Who would have guessed that some 20 years later their dream would still be alive and growing. Making the transition from the "Lazy M Ranch", to the Lazy M Lodge, it was important to us that the spirit and energy that they developed would be carried on to become a place to make even more memories.

It is important to us to share their story....

BEGINNINGS OF THE LAZY M RANCH

by Margie and Lane Moore

A BIT OF HISTORY

The Lazy M was named after the ranch's cattle brand during the fluctuating cattle industry. To offset the roller coaster nature of agriculture, in 1990 Lane and Margie Moore opened their home and their way of life to guests from around the world. With Lane's sense of humour, and his talents as a horseman and instructor, and Margie's nurturing personality and business sense, the Lazy M was born.

Disclaimer: some names have been changed to respect guest privacy. The stories and poems are related here are my own interpretations. They are simply told to entertain.

Lazy M Ranch

Ranches in Western Canada have always been places where people could be sure of warm hospitality. No matter how many cowboys showed up on the doorstep, pioneer cooks were always ready to set one more place at the table. This tradition is one we are proud to continue, and it starts the moment you walk through the door.

Margie and Lane Moore

Building the Lodge

The almost finished Lodge

Aerial View of the Lazy M Ranch, 1992

A few years ago, we started to get interested in serving more traditional ranch food, so we asked friends and family for recipes and came up with a dandy collection of real Canadian comfort food. Some of these recipes have been used since the first homesteaders arrived in these parts. For a sample of "tried and true" Western food, you should take a look at our Branding Weekend menu.

For adventurous guests, we offer a stay at our tent camp in the mountains. Needless to say, after a day's riding in the Rockies, you will return to camp with a "mountain" of an appetite. But don't worry, the hearty Mountain Camp menu will satisfy your hunger.

We are fortunate to live in a part of Alberta, that produces some of the best beef in the world. Most of our recipes are simple ones that emphasize the delicious natural flavor of meat.

The Lazy M Ranch is perched on the banks of a pristine river called the North Raven (or Stauffer Creek). You can sit on the house deck and watch Brown Trout rise to hatch in the waters below. The Lazy M encourages sport fly fishing, and they are challenging and fun to catch, As a consolation for not catching one, however, we have "other fish to fry" on our Catch and Release menu.

In recent years, many folks have become vegetarian or just want to lighten up on their meat intake. In addition to serving lots of fresh veggies and salads with regular meals, we've come up with some excellent vegetarian recipes for our Grass Eaters menu.

There are "bits and bobs" scattered throughout the book. These mini recipes offer up little details that enhance meals and make them special.

We often have fifteen to twenty people around the big Lazy M dining table, so our recipes reflect this. They are adjustable for fewer servings.

We hope this little book brings warmth and a smile to your soul, just as the meals will bring comfort and Canadian ranch hospitality to your table.

THE LAZY M STORY

In the 90s after some years of the drought
We were seriously wonderin'
What's this ranching about?
Presented with Apricot Brandy
A Birthday surprise ...
You know when you're drinkin'
You're always so wise!
We've got the right spot,
The fish, horses & cows ...
Let's start us a Guest Ranch!
And that truly is how
The Lazy M Ranch came to be
Finding the guests
Will be a challenge, said he."

A PLACE TO MAKE MEMORIES

Well, think tourism,
Think Banff and Jasper
And folks from afar.
The Japanese are just what we're looking' for!
It didn't take long 'til we learned our mistake
Right under our nose was the market to make.
Our local Albertans, specially Edmonton town
Were people just wishin'
And lookin' down
To the spring-fed waters
Called Stauffer Creek.
The fishin' and ridin.'
They were anxious to take
A wee bit of a holiday …
Their worries and troubles,
The stress from their jobs
To put all on hold
And to stop for a pause!

The fresh air, the farm food,
The ranch family feel
Had guests comin' back
Year after year!
We offer them comfort,
Riding, mountains and more
In turn they have given us stories galore.
We've travelled the world over
Never leaving our door!

So, sit back, curl up and give this a look
'cause some of those stories are here
In this book!

SUN TEA

Warmth and western hospitality greet guests upon arrival. Coffee, tea, drinks and treats are served. On warm days the wrap-around deck invites visitors to sink into a chair, breathe deeply, start to unwind, and sip a glass of sun tea.

Take a large glass jar (large pickle or mayonnaise jars are great).

Fill ¾ full with water, then place 5 or 6 black or herbal tea bags in it.

Place the lid on tightly and set in a sunny spot (ours goes on the deck).

Steep outside for a long, hot day.

Add sliced lemons or oranges and refrigerate.

With their sun tea, guests might enjoy Tart-less Butter Squares.

TART-LESS BUTTER SQUARES

BASE:
1¼ cup flour
½ cup butter or margarine
½ cup brown sugar

FILLING:
1/3 cup butter or margarine
2 tbsp milk or cream
1 tsp vanilla
1 cup currants or raisins
1 cup brown sugar
1 egg, beaten
1 tbsp flour
1 tbsp vinegar

Preheat oven to 350°

Press base ingredients into a small square pan and bake for 15 minutes. Mix filling ingredients together and spread over the base. Return to the oven and bake for 20 more minutes.

Branding time at the Lazy M

BRANDING WEEKEND AT THE LAZY M

The lifetime Lazy M brand identifies all Moore cattle and was assigned to Lane by the Department of Agriculture. It is described as "L Lazy Left M over a half Diamond." It must be placed on the animal's right hip.

The Lazy M brands cattle every spring on the Victoria Day Long Weekend in May. This coincides with the local Caroline Rodeo, Parade and Cabaret. The herd is rounded up, the calves separated and pushed through a chute into a calf squeeze where they are inoculated, branded and checked for general health. The Lazy M uses this method, so everyone can participate in three busy, fun-filled, "working" days.

LANE'S FAMOUS PANCAKES

It's not often you will see the "master horseman" in the kitchen, whipping up a frothy batter and pouring perfectly uniform, golden hot cakes on the griddle. This Branding Day recipe has accompanied many guests to all parts of the world.

2 cups flour
2 cups milk
3 eggs
1 tbsp sugar
pinch of salt
1 tsp white vinegar
1 tsp baking soda
3 tsp baking powder
4 tsp cooking oil
1 tsp vanilla

Lane's secret is to whisk the batter well. It should not be too thin, nor too thick. Make sure the griddle is hot before you pour, and turn your pancake only once, after bubbles appear on the raw side.

Serve Lane's pancakes with MacGregor Syrup

MACGREGOR SYRUP

1 cup brown sugar

Add enough heavy cream and blend so that the mixture is the colour of light toffee.

Cook in microwave on high for 2 minutes. Stir and cook again for 1 minute. Remove from microwave and add 1 tsp of vanilla. Stir and serve hot on pancakes.

Shannon MacGregor was our "Sunshine" wrangler for four years. She was the best person to cook for, as every meal was her favourite. She never failed to give accolades to the cooks and her hearty thanks always made Ranch cooking fun.

Her grandmother's "secret syrup" is not only great on pancakes, it can be used in coffee, poured on popcorn, as a dip for your strawberries. It really is a "low-calorie," multipurpose syrup!

Shannon loved the children who visited and we know she will be the best teacher ever! Many of our little guests have provided us with great stories over the years.

BARANT & MATILDA

The very first guests who came to our door
Were folks camping from Prince Rupert – their children 7 & 4.
Barant, the oldest was precocious and wise
Wee Matilda was serious & small in her size
Lane took them out riding
Barant had his own horse
Matilda rode with Lane
For wee ones, just a matter of course
Up to the cows they went for their ride
They stopped at the bulls, as Lane was the guide.
When Barant quizzed Lane on "those parts hanging under the bull"
Lane's answer was serious, the truth he would tell.
"Those are their testicles. You know what that means?"
And Barant said: "Yes", Lane knew he was keen.
But shy Matilda piped up from out of the blue ...
"Mine don't hang down so far – but I have some too!"

Lunch on branding day follows the sorting and separating of the cows and calves. It is generally not a heavy meal. This cauliflower soup is enough to "stick with" the cowpokes during the afternoon's branding.

CREAMY CAULIFLOWER SOUP

Every time we make soups they are a little different because we increase or decrease quantities depending on the group size, as well as adding, deleting or altering ingredients. Therefore, our soup recipes are simply guidelines.

1 onion, chopped
1 clove garlic, crushed
2 tbsp chicken or veggie bouillon, dissolved in 2 cups HOT water.
3-4 large potatoes (depending on the crowd)
1 cauliflower, chopped
1-2 more cups water
1 tbsp each of sugar, salt and pepper
pinch of basil and red pepper flakes.
1-2 cans evaporated milk or 1-2 cups half-and-half cream
2-4 tbsp Cheese Whiz

Fry bacon with chopped onion and garlic. When browned, add chicken bouillon with hot water. Cook potatoes and cauliflower in this stock until very tender. Mash with potato masher. Add 1-2 cups more of water to thick and creamy consistency and season with basil, red pepper flakes. Simmer and stir. Do not boil. Add evaporated milk or cream, sugar salt and pepper. Add Cheese Whiz before serving and garnish with parsley flakes.

FRESH SPRING RHUBARB PUDDING

To top off branding lunch we often serve this dessert.

6 cups chopped rhubarb
1 small package strawberry Jello powder
1 cup of sugar
2 eggs, beaten
1 tsp vanilla
1 cup milk,
2 cups flour
2 tsp baking powder
½ tsp salt
sugar and cinnamon to taste

Preheat oven to 350°

Combine rhubarb and Jello in the bottom of a greased 9 x 13 baking dish. Cream margarine with sugar. Add beaten eggs, milk, vanilla. Separately, mix flour, baking powder and salt and add to wet ingredients for batter. Spread over rhubarb mixture and top with sprinkled sugar and cinnamon. Bake for 50-60 minutes. Serve warm with ice cream.

DARLENE & JOHN

We have good neighbours, namely Darlene and John
This here's one of their stories – it ain't all that long.

'Twas in the spring as all of you Ranchers know – it's the prime ...
When lots of the new calves get sick, need treating' & taking' the time,
From sun-up til sun-down you're out and about
Checking' little asses for sick bloody scours and 'gout'!

John found one, a sick one – darn near flat out
But you know when you walk up – new life they discover
They can buck like a young deer, searching' for cover!
This here calf was sickly, that John could tell
So up to the house he went to solicit some help!

Now farmers and ranchers wouldn't be where they're at
Without a good wife to help and to always be there
On call, day or night, in any weather – be it foul or fair!
Darlene, being a good wife for her John that is true
She was up in a flash and told John just what to do!

"I'll just jump in that old truck, its faster of course
Than catching old chaos, and saddling' that horse!
We'll drive down real slow and you can sit on the hood
Then rope that little calf and treat it up good!"

Well, they bounced, and they wandered all over that field
'Til John spied the sick calf and yelled "turn on some speed"!
She followed real close as he twirled on his rope ...
He let fly with accuracy – (a prayer and a hope)!

He caught that calf on his very first toss
And Darlene thinking' that she was his boss...
Well, she slammed to a halt, as a good roping' horse does
She forgot that the bug screen, a brace that it was
The only thing holding her husband atop
When she stomped those brakes causing that real sudden stop ...
John went a flying' by leaps and by bounds
Why he hardly was touching' his feet to the ground!
That calf was a travelling' as fast as he might
John was launched, couldn't stop – try as he'd like!

When finally, that calf drug John, got tired then stopped
John treated him calmly and then undid his rope.
He walked back to the truck with firm lip and got in
But couldn't help notice, Darlene with a grin ...
Then the humour arose from out of that cab
John just had to laugh – he couldn't stay mad!

The picture it paints in my mind to this day
Is a pleasure I relish and enjoy when I lay
Back and wonder what's this ranching' about?
I know it's the little things, the daily routine
That we all can find fun with and appreciate being
Out here in the country, where birth, dying and such
Is part of a great scheme – we all love so much!

THE STAUFFER CREEK

The Lazy M is perched on the banks of a pristine little river called North Raven or Stauffer Creek. Famous (or infamous to many) this spring-fed creek has been labelled the Ph.D. of fly fishing streams. If a sport fisherman can catch fish in the Stauffer, he is almost certainly guaranteed to catch fish anywhere.

The rate of flow (4,000 gallons per minute), the gravel beds, deep holes and diverse insects have made this creek Brown Trout heaven. Noted as one of Alberta's top Brown Trout spawning streams, this creek simply appears from out of the ground only two miles from the ranch. Stocked way back in the 30's there are now approximately 1,000 fish per mile.

Come spring, Stauffer is the first fishable stream in this part of the province. When other creeks and rivers are muddy for weeks due to rain and runoff, the Stauffer clears in only a day or two. It truly is what Lane calls 'a million dollar' stream!

Because the North Raven is predominately a sport stream, we offer other seafood choices on the ranch menus.

STAUFFER CROWD-PLEASER TUNA CASSEROLE

1 large Costco tin of tuna, drained
3 onions, chopped
10 stalks of celery, chopped
3 cups mixed vegetables (broccoli, cauliflower, carrots, steamed or frozen)
1½ lbs. frozen peas
2 tins mushrooms
3 tins cream of mushroom soup
3 cups milk
3 cups grated cheddar cheese
2 cups minute rice
1/3 cup melted butter
2 cups cornflakes
salt and pepper

Preheat oven to 325°

Combine all these ingredients with the tuna and place in a large casserole dish or baking pan. We often use leftover veggies – but the broccoli is a must. Any creamed soup will suffice. Leftover cooked rice can be substituted for Minute Rice. Mix together cornflakes and butter and spread on top of casserole. Bake large casserole for 1 hour. Yield: 15 servings. Freezes well. Serve with green salad

LEAFY LETTUCE SALAD

variety of lettuces, torn
toasted almonds
toasted pine nuts
1 tin mandarin oranges, drained

DRESSING:
1 cup olive oil
¼ cup balsamic vinegar
½ tsp sugar (to taste)

Toast nuts in butter and sugar to slightly candy them. Cool before tossing with lettuce and mandarin sections. Drizzle dressing over just before serving

BAKED SALMON

MARINADE:

1 tbsp brown sugar

½ cup rye whiskey

1 tbsp molasses

½ cup oil

2 tbsp soy sauce

2 cloves of garlic, crushed

salt and pepper

TO BAKE SALMON:

Preheat oven to 350°

Marinate for at least one hour. Cover the inside of the whole fish with salt (learned this from a Japanese guest). Seal tightly in tin foil and bake. When done, remove skin, split fish down the back and open. Separate and remove bones (they should easily separate intact). Arrange on a platter with lemon wedges and parsley for garnish. Serve with green salad.

SALMON/ FISH SAUCE

1 cup sour cream
1 cup yogurt
2 tbsp sweet relish
½ tsp each Tabasco and ketchup
4 tbsp lemon juice with zest
chopped capers and dill weed to taste

Mix altogether and serve like tartar sauce with baked fish.

Rice dishes just go with fish. Here are a couple of good ones.

RICE PILAF

1 cup long grain rice
1 cup pearl barley
¼ cup butter
8 green onions, chopped
2 10 oz. tins consommé
2 tins water
1 tin whole mushrooms with liquid

Preheat oven to 350°

Brown rice and barley in butter until golden. Add onion, consommé, water and mushrooms

Cook in covered casserole for 1 hour or until liquid is absorbed. Fluff with fork and serve. Can be frozen and reheated. Yield: 8-10 servings.

CURRIED RICE

½ cup rice
2 cups warm water
1 chopped onion
1 tbsp curry powder
1 can tomatoes
2 Tbsp. melted butter
salt and pepper

Preheat oven to 350°

Soak rice in water for ¾ hour. Add onion, curry powder, tomatoes. Salt and pepper to taste. Bake 1 ½ hours, stirring occasionally. Stir in melted butter and serve.

Another old time favourite completes a seafood meal!

PINEAPPLE DELIGHT

2½ cups graham wafer crumbs
½ cup melted butter
¼ tsp cinnamon
1½ cups icing sugar
½ cup softened butter
2 eggs
1 14 oz. can crushed pineapple, drained
1 cup whipped cream (whipped)

Preheat oven to 325°

Mix crumbs, cinnamon and butter. Press ½ of the mixture into a greased 9 x13 pan. Bake for 20 minutes. Cool. Beat the sugar, butter and eggs well and spread over base. Fold pineapple into whipped cream and top with remaining crumb mixture. Refrigerate at least 4 hours before serving.

THE MOUNTAIN CAMP

The Mountain Camp came about as a bonus for so many guests who returned year after year. We wanted to share more of Alberta with these folks. The West Country and the mountains beckoned. Not only do we have a 5 Star Base Camp, we also boast an "Outpost" camp that offers guests even more mountain riding.

Covered wagon on the way to the mountain camp

Margie and Lane in the Wagon

Mountain Camp accommodations

Time around the campfire at mountain camp

CARSON'S STORY

Many Cowboys have been 'born' at the Lazy M. One of them was Carson, who fulfilled a dream here.

Carson was a night watchman in London. Even our British guests had a hard time understanding his accent. The western story books he had read as an adolescent in the evenings inspired his passion and informed his abilities. It was impressive though that through travel agents, Carson had travelled North America fulfilling his Cowboy Dreams.

Carson sauntered down the stairs as if he had stepped from the pages of a Zane Grey novel, with leather chaps and gloves, a big belt buckle, a dandy shirt, long rider cat, a long silk bandanna (that Lane said could easily have been used for a hanging) and a large felt hat. He sat down at the breakfast table, removing nothing but his hat. With food flying and lips smacking, he inhaled his meal in minutes--and he was ready to ride.

Out in the corral, we discerned that although Carson had been to quite a few ranches, he was still petrified of horses. His riding ability and horsemanship skills were challenged, to say the least. Carson had to be boosted up every time he mounted, and each time Lane gave him a helping hand up, the effort caused Carson to pass wind! Thank goodness for a sense of humour and a steady horse.

We got him up on Esther, our Appaloosa, who gets 'em all! We had to bring the cow herd home and

we knew that on Esther, Carson would be safe and out of harm's way (and ours too)!

The herd was easy to round up and once on the road we simply had to keep them moving. Carson was 'way behind while Esther calmly plodded along, stopping often to munch the roadside grasses. He shouted his best "yippee tiy yiy yays" and beat loudly on his leather chaps. The cattle moved without incident, and Carson was one happy cow pusher.

One rainy afternoon, six of us piled into the big Dodge for a shopping trip into Rocky Mountain House. Carson squeezed in--as always, dressed in full regalia. We turned up the music and after just one verse Carson was singing along with Ian Tyson and Marty Robbins.

Shopping was an event for Carson He bought more bandannas, more gloves and more western paraphernalia, but when he tried to climb into the truck with his brand new spurs jingling on his boots, one of the guests advised him to remove them before he tripped or got tangled up. It was also suggested that the spurs would be just fine for show, but that Esther would probably not share the same appreciation for them as he did.

On another occasion while out on the trail, Carson let Esther walk under a low tree branch. Carson was not into "taking control," nor capable of the fine art of "steering," so he bounced off and landed with a solid "oomph!" Sarah, a policewoman from Dorset, was helping wrangle that day and simply "lost it" on poor old Carson. She yanked him onto his feet, jerked the long rider coat from his back (it was very warm that day), threw him back up on Esther and told him he had to take some of his "God damn clothes off so as to have some strength left to ride and manage his horse!" It was probably a good thing he had so many clothes on--great padding, easier landing.

Although Carson's table manners made everyone shudder (he did love to eat), his enthusiasm for working with the cattle and the passion he showed for the cowboy lifestyle softened our hearts and

everyone, even Sarah, looked out for Carson and made certain that both he and Esther had a good time.

After doing most of the work for ourselves for over seven seasons, Lane and I began to "burn out." Thoughts of selling came over us. We tried, but fortunately no deals were successful. Then we took a deep breath, regrouped, and decided to hire more help. Eleanor Pengelly seemed the answer to my prayers, and she would cook for us for three years.

MY ANGEL

October 1999

Everyone has one – I'm convinced of that
An Angel is what I'm speaking about.
The first seven years, I'd done most of the cooking
But the spring of '99 for help I was looking!
I'd been spreading the word in village and town
Getting closer to start up and no one was found!

Well, one day out of the blue
A phone call for me – for a job interview.
A most pleasant voice was asking of me
"Do you need help cooking, I'm interested", said she.
The next afternoon came a knock at the door
A sweet smile, kind eyes and a mane of hair men adore –
There stood my angel – her name was Eleanor!

For three seasons we worked hard
We cooked and we cleaned
Eleanor a treasure, like I'd never seen.
Side by side in the kitchen we laughed and we cried
A good friend she was to me, without even trying.
The cooking was fun but the joy that I'll treasure
Is the friendship that grew, for that there's no measure.

ELEANOR'S CHEESE MUFFINS

4½ cups flour
6 tbsp sugar
3 tbsp baking powder
1½ tsp salt
4½ cups sharp cheddar cheese
3 eggs
3 cups milk
¾ cup oil

Preheat oven to 400°

Mix all dry ingredients and cheese together. Mix wet ingredients and add to dry.
Bake for 20–25 minutes on a greased cookie sheet.

Many thanks to Margie and Lane for their story in bringing the Lazy M to life, and we are happy to be able to continue their dream. ...

- As the sun sets at the Lazy M Lodge

ONCE ONE PASSES THROUGH THE ENTRY
GATES OF TIME AND SPACE, IT MAY BE
HANDY TO KNOW THAT SIMPLY DWELLING
UPON JOY, ABUNDANCE, OR ANYTHING ELSE
INVOLVING PEOPLE, WILL LITERALLY DRAW
COMPLETE STRANGERS INTO YOUR LIFE, AS
IF THEY WERE PUPPETS ON MARIONETTE
STRINGS. CREATING NEW AND TOTALLY
UNPREDICTABLE CIRCUMSTANCES THAT
WILL BRING YOU MORE, MORE, MORE OF
WHATEVER YOU WERE THINKING ABOUT.

ABOUT THE AUTHOR

RANDY MCGHEE WAS RAISED ON THE FAMILY farm not far from Drumheller Alberta. The farm life for him helped build his character and life there was great. Grades 1-6 was in a one room school house. He was involved in the Presbyterian church, and local 4-H clubs, community involvement was important for him. He wrote articles for the local news paper as well as being involved in writing the community history book.

Once he finished high school, he followed his interest in carpentry work and got married, and started a family.

When he faced some life changes and embraced new challenges he felt his story needed to be told. Writing down his story and having support from his partner and guests the book came to life.

Now living and working the guest lodge business and enjoying their country.

CPSIA information can be obtained
at www.ICGtesting.com
Printed in the USA
LVHW020308270619
622469LV00002B/2/P

9 781525 543433